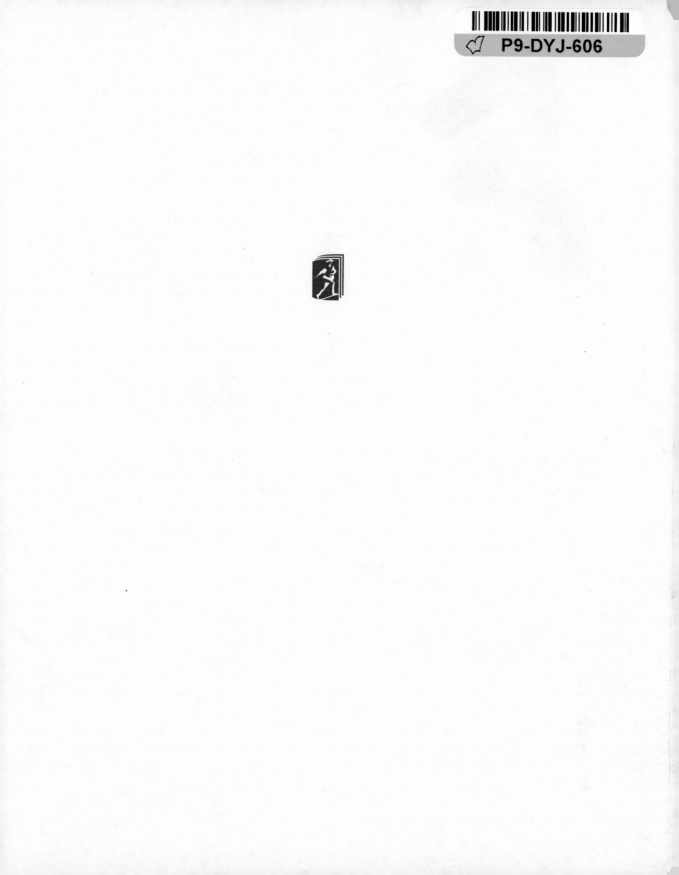

More Than 120 Inexpensive

Recipes for Great Meals from

America's Best-Known Chefs

TEXT AND RECIPES EDITED BY

Andrew Friedman

Chef on a Shoestring

SIMON & SCHUSTER PAPERBACKS

New York   London   Toronto   Sydney

SIMON & SCHUSTER PAPERBACKS
Rockefeller Center
1230 Avenue of the Americas
New York, NY 10020

First Simon & Schuster paperback edition 2004

SIMON & SCHUSTER PAPERBACKS and colophon are registered trademarks
of Simon & Schuster, Inc.

The recipes for Walter Staib's Salmon Corn Cakes (page 32), Walter Staib's Cucumber and Cream Salad (page 59), and Walter Staib's Curried French Lentil Salad and Sausage (page 68) are adapted from recipes in *The City Tavern Cookbook*, copyright © 1999 by Walter Staib, published by Running Press Book Publishers, Philadelphia and London.

The recipes for Michael Romano's Warm Shrimp and Bean Salad with Arugula (page 65), Michael Romano's Eggplant Parmigiana (page 115), and Michael Romano's Panna Cotta (page 214) were created by Michael Romano of Union Square Café and are used with the permission of Mr. Romano. The recipe for Michael Romano's Panna Cotta (page 214) is from *The Union Square Café Cookbook*, published by HarperCollins Publishers, Inc. Copyright © 1994 by Danny Meyer and Michael Romano.

The recipes for Michael Lomonaco's Basic Pasta Dough (page 97), Michael Lomonaco's Fresh Homemade Pasta with Wild Mushrooms (page 99), Michael Lomonaco's Pan-Roasted Halibut with Spring Vegetables (page 137), Michael Lomonaco's Chile-Rubbed Beef Pot Roast (page 176), Michael Lomonaco's Marinated and Grilled Pork Medallions (page 185), Michael Lomonaco's Quince Fruit Mustard (page 195), Michael Lomonaco's Mustard and Mint Beet Salad (page 197), and Michael Lomonaco's Flourless Chocolate-Walnut Brownie Torte (page 222) are copyright © 1997 Michael Lomonaco, all rights reserved.

The recipe for Jamie Shannon's Crawfish Boil (page 149) is from *Commander's Kitchen*, by Ti Martin and Jamie Shannon, copyright © 2000 by Commander's Palace, Inc. Used by permission of Broadway Books, a division of Random House, Inc.

The recipe for The American Heart Association's Spicy Grilled Chicken (page 162) is from *The New American Heart Association Cookbook*, by The American Heart Association. Copyright © 1998 by American Heart Association. Reprinted by permission of Times Books, a division of Random House, Inc.

Designed by Katy Riegel
Manufactured in the United States of America
1   3   5   7   9   10   8   6   4   2

The Library of Congress has cataloged the hardcover edition as follows:
Chef on a shoestring / more than 120 delicious, easy-on-the-budget recipes from
America's best chefs / text and recipes edited by Andrew Friedman.
p. cm.
Includes index.
1. Low budget cookery.   I. Friedman, Andrew.
TX652 .C4873 2001
641.5'52—dc21   00-046327

ISBN 0-7432-0072-1
0-7432-1143-X (Pbk)

Acknowledgments

THE SATURDAY EARLY SHOW "Chef on a Shoestring" feature has become one of the most popular cooking segments on network television. But many hands helped create the recipe for that success.

I would like to acknowledge Andrew Heyward, President of CBS News, and Linda Mason, CBS Vice President of Public Affairs, for their support and encouragement, which went a long way in helping the batter rise.

As any chef will tell you, preparation is key, and in the slicing and dicing department Kelly Buzby and Jee Won Park have done a masterful job producing the "Chef on a Shoestring" segments. They have also been wonderful ambassadors to the culinary community. Our anchors and chief tasters Russ Mitchell and Thalia Assuras, and her predecessors, Dawn Stensland and Susan Molinari, have helped bring out the best in the chefs.

Presentation is so important in making the meal look appetizing. I would like to thank Victor Paganuzzi and George McGarvey for their excellent work in creating and decorating the set. In the short-order department, where timing is everything, we have master chefs in director Bill Brady and senior producer Ann Yih.

I am also grateful to two people who helped create the recipe for this book, senior editor Sydny Miner and the writer, Andrew Friedman.

Last, and most important, I would like to thank the chefs for their generosity of spirit, their time, and their amazing abilities to create so many wonderful three-course meals for just twenty bucks.

Hal Gessner
Executive Producer, CBS Saturday Early Show

I would like to dedicate this book

to the staff and crew of *The Saturday Early Show,*

because they have taught me the

meaning of dedication.

—Hal Gessner

Executive Producer

Contents

FINGER FOODS AND SMALL PLATES   29

Mario Batali's Mushroom and White Bean Bruschetta ⌐ Walter Staib's Salmon Corn Cakes ⌐ Eric Ripert's Stuffed Tomatoes ⌐ Amanda Hesser's Creamy Leeks and Tarragon on Toast ⌐ John Schenk's Buffalo Chicken Wings ⌐ John Schenk's Clementine Cheese Fondue with Toasted Baguette ⌐ Don Pintabona's Prosciutto-Wrapped Figs with Smoked Mozzarella ⌐ Don Pintabona's Caramelized Onion, Gorgonzola, and Rosemary Pizza ⌐ Erica Miller's Tuna Carpaccio ⌐ Richard Sandoval's Mahi

Mahi Ceviche ⁓ Richard Krause's Grilled Mozzarella and Tomato ⁓ Mario Batali's Marinated Roasted Peppers with Goat Cheese, Olives, and Fett'unta ⁓ Jeanette Maier's Stuffed Portobello Mushrooms ⁓ Peter Kelly's Roasted Onions with Bacon and Apple Stuffing ⁓ Thomas Salamunovich's Smoked Salmon with Crisp Onion Rings, Grilled Asparagus, and Pea Shoots ⁓ Alfred Portale's Creamy Polenta with Cremini Mushrooms ⁓ Sara Moulton's Quiche Lorraine

SALADS   53

Erik Blauberg's Baby Arugula Greens with Watermelon "Croutons" and Caesar Dressing ⁓ John Schenk's Classic Caesar Salad ⁓ Aaron Bashy's Braised Leek Salad ⁓ Walter Staib's Cucumber and Cream Salad ⁓ Bill Wavrin's Spinach and Red Onion Salad ⁓ Ira Freehof's Hearts of Lettuce with Blue Cheese Dressing ⁓ John Villa's Boston Lettuce Salad with Green Beans and Lemongrass Dressing ⁓ Nick Stellino's Mushroom Salad ⁓ Marcus Samuelsson's Asparagus and Bean Sprout Salad with Dill Pesto ⁓ Michael Romano's Warm Shrimp and Bean Salad with Arugula ⁓ Kerry Heffernan's Roasted Root Vegetable Salad ⁓ Walter Staib's Curried French Lentil Salad and Sausage ⁓ Terrance Brennan's Roasted Beet Salad with Arugula and Aged Goat Cheese ⁓ Terrance Brennan's Pear and Gorgonzola Salad

SOUPS AND STEWS 73

PASTA AND RISOTTO 95

Vegetarian Main Courses 113

Michael Romano's Eggplant Parmigiana ∼ Bill Wavrin's Mushroom Potato Burgers ∼ Jeanette Maier's Hearty Root Vegetable and Lentil Stew with Three Herbs ∼ Brian Whitmer's Baked Polenta with Rosemary Roasted Portobello Mushrooms and Winter Tomato Sauce ∼ David Walzog's Black Bean Casserole ∼ David Walzog's Asparagus and Cremini Mushroom Barley "Risotto"

Fish and Seafood 125

Amanda Hesser's Mussels with Garlic and Fresh Herbs ∼ Erik Blauberg's Spanish Mackerel with Sautéed Potatoes, Cremini Mushrooms, and Spicy Tomatoes ∼ Eric Ripert's Shrimp Tabbouleh ∼ Alfred Portale's Cod with Brussels Sprouts, Yukon Gold Potatoes, and Onions ∼ Rick Moonen's Salmon Burgers with Green Tartar Sauce ∼ Paul Opitz's Bay Scallops and Crab Meat à la Chesapeake ∼ Michael Lomonaco's Pan-Roasted Halibut with Spring Vegetables ∼ David Reardon's Pan-Seared Scallops and Oyster Mushroom Sweet Potato Salad with Cilantro Ginger Vinaigrette ∼ Henry Meer's Brook Trout Steamed with Vegetables ∼ Tom Douglas's Crispy Fried Snapper with Chile Ponzu ∼ Marcus Samuelsson's Horseradish-Baked Salmon with Carrot-Ginger Broth and Mussels ∼ Richard Vellante's Polenta-Crusted Salmon with Fall Vegetables and Chestnuts ∼ Kerry

Heffernan's Skate with Sautéed Beet Greens and Boiled Potatoes ⁓ Joseph Tucker's Tuna Sambuca ⁓ Jamie Shannon's Crawfish Boil

POULTRY 151

Jim Botsacos's Lemon Garlic Roasted Chicken ⁓ Joseph T. Bonanno, Jr.'s Grilled Stuffed Chicken ⁓ Michael Lomonaco's Chicken Fricassee ⁓ Lou Piuggi's Moroccan Chicken Tagine with Couscous ⁓ Scott Campbell's Stuffed Chicken Legs with Mushroom Stuffing ⁓ Terrance Brennan's Chicken Piccata with Cauliflower, Capers, Sage, and Orange ⁓ Charlie Palmer's Seared Chicken Breast with Red Onion Vinaigrette ⁓ The American Heart Association's Spicy Grilled Chicken ⁓ Waldy Malouf's Cold Herbed Roast Chicken with Marinated Japanese Pear Tomatoes ⁓ Spinach-Stuffed Chicken Breast with Mushroom Sauce ⁓ John Doherty's Roast Breast and Braised Legs of Chicken with Olive and Lemon Potatoes and String Beans ⁓ Alfonso Contrisciani's Pepper-Crusted Turkey "London Broil" with Mushroom Confit ⁓ Ray Arpke's Turkey Breast Scaloppine with Mushrooms and Mustard Butter Sauce

DESSERTS   205

BASICS   225

Foreword

IN THE HOURS BEFORE SUNRISE on Saturday mornings, midtown Manhattan is a dark and desolate place. If you walked the streets at 5 A.M., you might wonder whether New York really deserved the nickname "the city that never sleeps." But there are signs of life even in these wee hours—a few errant cab drivers, deli-counter people, regally attired doormen, and the crew of the CBS News program that I've been producing since 1997.

All television shows evolve over the years and ours is no exception; we've even changed the title from the original *CBS News Saturday Morning* to *The Saturday Early Show*. But there's one component of the program that's been a constant since the first morning we took to the airwaves—the weekly segment called "Chef on a Shoestring" on which we invite a well-known restaurant chef or food personality to prepare a three-course meal for four on a budget.

The concept for "Chef on a Shoestring" grew organically from our formative days of a show on a shoestring; when the broadcast was first conceived, we were short on money, personnel, and time. It seems amazing in hindsight, but we had just two and one-half months to pull the whole thing together.

Cooking segments are an unofficial prerequisite for weekend morning shows, and when it came time to devise ours, I found myself taking a self-pitying view of my own understaffed and time-starved circumstances. But then a delicious idea hit me—put a chef in similar straits and see what happens. "Chef on a Shoestring," I whispered to myself, and the segment was on its way.

Of course, I didn't want just *any* chefs. I wanted the best chefs the city—and the country—had to offer. And their response was gratifying. Most of the chefs have appeared on other shows and in numerous print articles and, of course, they create food in the country's best restaurants. But this was a new challenge for them—one as it turned out they were eager to meet.

At our next staff meeting, I ran the "Chef on a Shoestring" concept by the staff hoping that a producer would want to take it on. A young associate named Kelly Buzby modestly offered to "give it a shot." Well, her first shot ended up setting the tone for what today, three years later, remains the model every Saturday. For our fast-approaching first week, Kelly lined up Michael Lomonaco, who ran the kitchen at the '21' Club and now has a show (*Epicurious*) on the Discovery Channel and is at Windows on the World. This was the first real test. We gave Michael just $20 and sent him to the Union Square Greenmarket to purchase the ingredients as our camera watched. This shopping trip became the signature opening of "Chef on a Shoestring." (I have to point out that the segment is currently produced by the equally talented Jee Park.)

For our debut on September 13, 1997, Michael demonstrated how to make Tomato and Basil Salad and Chicken Fricassee; he served apples and cheese for dessert. At the end of the show, our cohost Russ Mitchell invited viewers to write in for the recipe. The following week, we got our first inkling of how popular this segment would be as bag after bag of mail came pouring in. Our staff and interns gradually worked their way through the piles, sending printed recipes to viewers around the country. It was a phenomenon that grew every week, and continues to grow today. Eventually we began posting the recipes on our Web site, but—even though we get 100,000 hits per week—the letters continue to pour in. And we love it.

The "Chef on a Shoestring" TV segment reflects the times in which we live and, by extension, the times in which we cook. Though the economy (at least at the time of this writing) is booming, I still think that people generally feel on the losing end of things. We all seem to have less and less free time, and sometimes we feel we're getting less for our money, whether it's in diminished service or the quantity and quality of the goods we buy. When the chef of an upscale restaurant shows up on our program, shopping in a regular supermarket or grocery store and then preparing uncommonly accessible recipes, delivers something that is too often lacking in our lives today: value. In the fall of 2001, the $20 budget was increased to $30, which maintains the broadcast's goal of presenting an affordable, gourmet three-course meal for four people.

Thanks to this segment, we've been privileged to meet and work with some of the most respected chefs in the country. They have graciously donated their time, creativity, and personality to our show. The budget may be on a shoestring, but our chefs have done everything to ensure that the recipes in this book are rich in every other way.

Hal Gessner
Executive Producer
The Saturday Early Show
April 2000, New York City

A Message from Share Our Strength

DEAR FRIENDS OF "Chef on a Shoestring":

Share Our Strength began in the basement of a row house on Capitol Hill in 1984. We started with the belief that everyone has a "strength" to share in the fight against hunger and poverty. At first, we organized a handful of chefs to cook for fundraisers. Then restaurateurs and culinary professionals jumped in to help. As word spread about our anti-hunger events, new ideas emerged. Writers offered to contribute their works for benefit anthologies. Illustrators came up with ideas for children's books.

Today we mobilize thousands of creative professionals. In the culinary industry, individuals organize events, host dinners, and teach cooking and nutrition classes to low-income families. Literary professionals conduct benefit readings and contribute works to Share Our Strength books. To bring even more resources to the fight, we develop creative partnerships with a range of industries and cause-related campaigns and product sales to promote social change.

As a result, we have raised more than $84 million since 1984 for our efforts to stamp out hunger and poverty. We're fueled by a simple but powerful philosophy: *It takes more than food to fight hunger.* It takes each one of us, sharing our strengths, to break the cycle.

By buying this book, you share your strength with your community, because all royalties from the purchase of *Chef on a Shoestring* will be donated to Share Our Strength. By making this purchase, you will be making a real difference in the lives of thousands of people across America.

I thank you for your support of Share Our Strength and wish you good cooking!

Sincerely,
Bill Shore
Founder and Executive Director
Share Our Strength

Introduction

IF THERE'S ONE thing you don't expect to find in a cookbook, it's a moral. But there's definitely a moral to the "Chef on a Shoestring" story: It's possible to cook deeply satisfying food on a very low budget. In the pages that follow, you'll encounter recipes from a great many chefs who have happily and creatively met our challenge to cook a three-course dinner for four on a budget of $20. In doing so, these chefs have provided us with not only inspiration but also a great deal of information. We've tried to capture everything they've brought to the table on *The Saturday Early Show*—their shopping tips, their recipes, and their personalities.

Rather than reprint complete menus from a small number of chefs, we've selected a greater cross-section of cooking talents and arranged this book according to conventional recipe chapters. In doing so, we've been able to include recipes from more than 50 chefs, allowing you to sample the sensibility and taste sensations that have made each of them a success.

Shopping on a Shoestring

A few universal truths have emerged over the three years of producing "Chef on a Shoestring." Among the most important talents required to cook successfully on a shoestring is strategic shopping. A few key tips:

DON'T OVERPURCHASE

The supermarket is a tempting place where the enormous variety invites you to spend, spend, spend. Try to buy only as much as you need to make a recipe, unless you have something else in mind for the same ingredients over the next day or two.

BUY IN-SEASON INGREDIENTS

This is one of the most effective ways of keeping your budget down; when fruits and vegetables are grown locally and needn't be shipped in from elsewhere, their costs drop substantially. So try to use ingredients at the peak of their season, such as tomatoes, corn, and eggplant in the summer; apples, pears, and root vegetables in the fall; and peas, asparagus, and stone fruits in the spring and early summer. Not only are these ingredients at their least expensive in season but also their most intense flavor.

BE RESOURCEFUL

If you develop the skill of using all parts of an ingredient, you'll be able to get the maximum value out of each and every one. For example, finding uses for herb stems or potato scraps, or knowing how to butcher and use all parts of a chicken, can be the first steps to real economy in the kitchen. Many of the chefs in this book have demonstrated how to do this, and if you pay close attention, you'll find endless applications for this resourcefulness in your own cooking.

Pantry

The word *pantry* has a quaint old-fashioned ring to it, but even as we tiptoe into the new millennium, no substitute has yet been devised for a well-stocked kitchen.

Think of the ingredients in your pantry as you would your collection of pots and pans, spoons and spatulas, knives and cutting board—as part of your roster of basics. Our guest chefs think of them that way, and one of the ground rules of shoestring cooking assumes that you have them on hand as well. If not it is impossible to make dinner for under $20. The olive oil, butter, salt, and pepper alone would run you close to that much.

Here are some key items no pantry should be without. Though a personalized kitchen will no doubt include additional spices, oils, mustards, and vinegars, this is a good basic list (in alphabetical order) and will have you prepared to cook any dish in this book.

BAY LEAVES

An aromatic leaf that imparts a slight, gentle pungency to sauces, stews, stocks, and soups. It's one of the imperative components of a bouquet garni or herb sachet. It's also one of the few herbs acceptable in its dried form, so there's no reason not to have them on hand.

BUTTER

Every recipe in this book, and most that you'll encounter elsewhere, calls for unsalted, or sweet, butter. The reason for this is elementary—it allows you to control the salt content of not only the overall dish but also each component in the recipe. (Butter isn't salted for flavor, but rather for preservation. If you freeze your butter before using it and finish any opened butter within a few weeks, there's no need to use salted unless you prefer the taste when used as a spread.)

CAPERS

Capers are the preserved flower buds of a shrub indigenous to Asia but which today is grown in other warm climates. Unpleasantly bitter when picked, capers are stored in vinegar or brine or packed in salt. They are a mainstay of classic French cooking and are employed especially in fish sauces. Be sure to rinse them well regardless of how they are stored before using them in any recipe.

CORNSTARCH

It doesn't turn up much in cooking these days, but cornstarch is one possible agent to call on for thickening a sauce or soup. It is first dissolved in warm water and then added to the cooking liquid. One of the benefits of using cornstarch for this purpose is that, unlike flour (which is often added earlier in the cooking process), the effects of cornstarch are immediately apparent, affording you more control over the thickness it produces. Another plus is that cornstarch produces a less cloudy result than other thickening agents.

DIJON MUSTARD

This assertively flavored French-style mustard is a must for many vinaigrettes and sauces.

DRIED HERBS AND SPICES

Dried herbs should generally be avoided for the simple reason that the flavor of fresh herbs is infinitely superior. (Two exceptions are oregano—which in dried form has a very appealing flavor—and bay leaves, which are described above.) For budgetary reasons, however, many of the chefs in this book have used dried herbs such as thyme and rosemary. Spices are another matter entirely. By all means stock your pantry with dried, ground spices such as allspice, cardamom, cinnamon, chili powder, cumin, ginger, saffron, and turmeric.

FLOUR

Unbleached all-purpose flour will get you through just about any cooking need, from making fresh pasta to baking a pie. But if you plan to make your own pasta you might want to keep some semolina flour on hand as well.

OILS

Canola oil

A neutral, multipurpose oil that holds up well over high temperatures. It's used for salad dressings and for sautéing.

Olive oil

Olive oil is another popular oil for sautéing. Extra-virgin olive oils come in a boundless array of varying fruitiness, body, and expense, and are often used as a condiment to dress a dish at the last minute. Become familiar with extra-virgin olive oils that have the qualities you seek.

Vegetable oil

Another neutral oil that may be used for sautéing when the flavor of the oil isn't an important consideration.

PEPPER

Almost every recipe in this book (except for desserts) indicates seasoning with freshly ground black pepper at some point. Pepper ground right from the mill has a heightened impact that preground commercial varieties are simply incapable of producing. Though the pomp of a peppermill being brought to the table seems more and more old-fashioned in restaurants with each passing year (as many restaurateurs have taken to placing small, do-it-yourself mills on the table), the sentiment is correct; if you want to offer your guests fresh pepper, place a small mill on the table rather than a shaker.

Also, in the spirit of this book, most recipes simply indicate black pepper, but it's a good idea to have two mills on hand, one with black and one with white pepper. Often you may interchange them, but there are times when the pungency of black pepper is a must (such as for seasoning cuts of meat) and other times when the inconspicuous appearance of white pepper is a plus (such as for seasoning clear soups or mashed potatoes).

SALT

Most of the savory recipes in this book call for at least some salt. Unless otherwise indicated, coarse kosher salt is a must—the results it produces are superior. Sea salt is a viable substitute, and where a particular chef has indicated sea salt, we've passed along the recommendation in his or her recipe. But if you don't have any sea salt, always feel free to use coarse salt.

As with pepper, you will usually be instructed to salt and pepper a recipe "to taste." This is among the most important steps in any recipe. If you don't yet have a developed sense of how to season for maximum impact, keep in mind that it's a fine line between perfectly seasoned and salty. Add and incorporate salt a little at a time and taste frequently until you achieve the desired result—which is usually a pronounced flavor of the ingredient being seasoned without an undue awareness of the salt itself.

Also note that even when a recipe indicates to "season to taste," you should not actually taste certain uncooked ingredients, such as uncooked chicken or pork. In these instances, the instruction simply means to season according to your own sensibility.

STARCHES (COUSCOUS, PASTA, RICE)

Grains and starches should be kept in your kitchen all times. While it's not necessary (or advisable, really) to have an extensive supply in your cupboard, you should probably keep some couscous, white and Arborio rice, and a variety of dried pasta in your pantry for last-minute meals. They not only show up in many recipes, but they're also wonderful last-minute mediums for improvisational cooking and a good way to use leftovers.

STOCKS

If you've never made your own stock, you'd be surprised how easy it is. Stock may be kept frozen for months. Many of the recipes in this book will be fine with canned, low-sodium broth or even water. There are also a few high-quality frozen stocks on the market these days. Stay away from bouillon cubes, which are overly salty and lack flavor.

SUGAR

For the most part, granulated sugar will get you through the recipes in this book. Occasionally, brown sugar and/or confectioner's sugar are called for, and so are worth having on hand as well.

TOMATOES (CANNED)

Though most chefs frown on canned vegetables, there are many high-quality canned tomatoes available and worth having in your cupboard year-round for last-minute sauces and to take the place of fresh tomatoes in the cold months. Find a brand you like and stick with it.

VINEGAR

For the most part, red wine vinegar is all you need for vinaigrettes and sauces, though it's worth having white wine vinegar on hand as well. Balsamic vinegar, the world-renowned elixir from Modena, Italy, is an extravagance that is usually appreciated in small quantities, so investing in a bottle will bring huge dividends. Be sure that you purchase only balsamic vinegar that's actually from Modena—most others are pale imitations.

WINE

Don't purchase so-called cooking wine for cooking, but instead buy an inexpensive dry wine such as Chardonnay or Cabernet Sauvignon. If making a pan sauce or wine sauce, it's often possible, and desirable, to use the wine you'll be drinking with your meal.

How to Use This Book

THIS BOOK IS ARRANGED in a fashion similar to most cookbooks you own. Following this introduction, you'll find recipe chapters divided into such subjects as Finger Foods and Small Plates, Salads, Pasta and Risotto, Poultry, Meats, and Desserts.

Although the chefs who cook on our show each produce a three-course menu (appetizer, main course, dessert), this book disperses their recipes into various categories in order to allow us to feature considerably more chefs in the book and to allow you to mix and match various courses from different chefs. Each chef's name appears with his or her recipes, and there's a collection of biographies in the back of the book that will tell you a bit about the chefs themselves.

THE RECIPES

Each recipe in this book features a headnote, which offers information such as the chef's inspiration for the dish and how it's been adjusted to suit the shoestring parameters.

As for the recipes themselves, the best advice is to read them all the way through at least once so that you're prepared for what's ahead. Though every effort has been made to forewarn you of any unexpected steps, it's a good idea to look and see if you need to have an ice bath ready or if you require a piece of equipment that you may not have.

BASICS

At the end of the book, you will find a few basic recipes. These are preparations and techniques, such as how to roast garlic or how to peel tomatoes, that appear over and over throughout the recipes.

Finger Foods and Small Plates

Mario Batali's Mushroom and White Bean Bruschetta

———

SERVES 4

Mario Batali is the ponytailed chef-proprietor (chef-general might be more accurate) behind a growing New York City restaurant empire that includes Babbo, Lupa, and Esca, with plans to culinarily conquer additional neighborhoods as well. Discussing his recipes, he exudes such effortless charisma, charm, and smarts that one gets the impression that if he hadn't discovered chefdom, he might have become the hippest history professor on the planet. Ask him about an Italian dish, and without a moment's hesitation, he fires off a historical and geographic context that adds intellectual interest to the most deceptively simple composition of ingredients. He even makes bruschetta beguiling, explaining that the name derives from the Italian word *buscare,* or "to cook over open coals," and refers to the toasted bread that forms the base of this starter.

This bruschetta evokes the white bean version Batali offers up at many of his outposts in New York. Among its attributes are that it may be reproduced over and over again with great consistency, a crucial quality in a restaurant dish and not a bad thing at home either.

4 tablespoons extra-virgin olive oil
10 ounces cremini mushrooms, trimmed, wiped clean with a damp cloth or paper towel, and quartered
2 tablespoons balsamic vinegar
1/2 teaspoon hot red pepper flakes
2 tablespoons thinly slivered basil leaves
1 clove garlic, thinly sliced
Coarse salt and freshly ground black pepper to taste
1 16-ounce can cannellini beans
8 1-inch-thick slices Italian peasant bread, toasted in the oven (preferably while cooking the mushrooms)

In a medium sauté pan, warm 2 tablespoons of the olive oil over moderate heat. Add the mushrooms to the pan and sauté for about 2 minutes until wilted.

In a mixing bowl, gently stir together the cooked mushrooms, remaining 2 tablespoons olive oil, the balsamic vinegar, red pepper flakes, basil, and garlic. Season lightly with salt and pepper.

Drain the water from the beans and gently mix them with the mushrooms. Arrange 2 warm toast slices on each plate. Divide the mushroom mixture evenly among the slices and serve.

Walter Staib's Salmon Corn Cakes

(*adapted from* The City Tavern Cookbook)

⁓

SERVES 4

Crab cakes are a beloved American standard, especially on the East Coast, where Maryland crab cakes are a summertime tradition. But Walter Staib, who was awarded the contract of Philadelphia's historic City Tavern in 1994, prefers a salmon cake with additional crunch and flavor contributed by fresh corn and bell pepper. Dill, the herb with which salmon has the greatest affinity, provides an aromatic dimension absent from crab cakes. You can also make smaller salmon corn cakes and serve them as a finger food.

2 ears fresh corn, husked and kernels cut from the cobs
Coarse salt to taste
1½ pounds fresh skinless, boneless salmon pieces
Freshly ground black pepper to taste
1 small onion, cut into ¼-inch dice
1 green bell pepper, seeded and finely diced
10–15 sprigs fresh dill, finely chopped
3 large egg yolks, at room temperature
¾ cup fine fresh bread crumbs
1 tablespoon fresh lemon juice
2 dashes Worcestershire sauce
3 dashes Tabasco sauce
4 tablespoons (½ stick) unsalted butter, at room temperature
2 tablespoons extra-virgin olive oil

Place the corn kernels in a small pot, cover with water, and season with salt. Cook over moderate heat for 5 to 8 minutes until the corn is heated through, being careful not to overcook. Remove from the heat, drain and reserve.

Fill a medium-size saucepan with enough water to cover the salmon pieces. Season the water with salt and pepper and bring it to a boil over high heat. Place the salmon pieces in the water, lower the heat, and simmer until the salmon is cooked, 4 to 5 minutes. Carefully drain the salmon pieces and set aside to cool.

In a medium-size mixing bowl, combine the corn, onion, green pepper, dill, egg yolks, bread crumbs, lemon juice, Worcestershire, and Tabasco. Break the salmon pieces into the mixing bowl and stir well, but gently, to incorporate. Form the mixture into 8 patties, placing them on a tray as they are formed. Refrigerate the cakes for 30 minutes to allow the salmon to set up a bit.

Preheat the oven to 350° F.

Remove the salmon from the refrigerator. Place the butter and oil in a large skillet over moderate heat. Melt the butter. Place the salmon cakes in the pan and brown both sides, 2 to 3 minutes per side, working in batches if you have to. Do not overcrowd the pan. Warm the salmon cakes on a sheet pan in the preheated oven for 10 minutes before serving.

Eric Ripert's Stuffed Tomatoes

S E R V E S   4

Based on his grandmother's recipe, Eric Ripert's stuffed tomatoes finds a filling of sausage, parsley, and bread crumbs served in the tomato itself, mirroring the presentation of its intended companion dish, the onion soup on page 88. Ripert, the executive chef of four-star seafood haven Le Bernardin, cautions home cooks to be careful not to scoop too close to the skin of the tomato or the "bowl" will break when cooked.

4 large beefsteak tomatoes
1 French roll, hard crust removed, cut into
    ¼-inch dice (about 3½ cups)
½ cup milk
12 ounces Italian pork sausage, casings
    removed
¼ cup roughly chopped flat-leaf parsley leaves
2 tablespoons chopped onion
1 teaspoon chopped garlic
1 large egg, at room temperature
¼ cup half-and-half
¼ teaspoon fine sea salt
2 pinches freshly ground white pepper

Amanda Hesser's Creamy Leeks and Tarragon on Toast

(adapted from The Cook and the Gardener, *W. W. Norton & Company, 1999)*

Preheat the oven to 350° F.

Slice ½ inch off the top of the tomatoes, leaving the stem intact. Reserve the tops to serve as lids. Scoop out the pulp and seeds of the tomatoes and reserve for another use.

Place the bread cubes in a bowl and cover with the milk. Combine the remaining ingredients in a separate mixing bowl. Squeeze the bread to remove the excess milk and add the bread to the ingredients in the other bowl. Stir to combine thoroughly.

Gently spoon equal portions of the bread mixture into the 4 tomatoes. Place the tomatoes in a baking dish.

Bake in the preheated oven for 25 minutes, then add ½ cup water to the pan. Continue to bake for another 25 minutes.

To serve, remove the stuffed tomatoes from the oven and top with the reserved tomato lids.

SERVES 4

New York Times food writer Amanda Hesser has a deep affection for leeks. She cooks with them year-round, the same frequency with which the French mentor at the center of her autobiographical book *The Cook and the Gardener* provided them. "I use leeks as much as I do garlic and onions," Hesser says of these sweet and delicate stalks. Having spent time working in Italy as well as France, she fashioned this dish as her answer to the ubiquitous Italian hors d'oeuvres—bruschetta. (See page 31 for a more traditional bruschetta recipe from Mario Batali.) According to Hesser, the contrast between the crispy toasted bread and the soft, cooked leeks never fails to surprise those who are tasting this appetizer for the first time. She also says that this dish will be delicious without the tarragon but believes that it's the use of this herb that really makes a difference.

Many bruschetta recipes instruct one to rub the bread with a cut garlic clove, but both Hesser and Batali prefer that you don't do this. Just one or two strokes of an uncut clove across the surface of each warm slice will imbue the toast with a faint garlic flavor.

2 medium leeks, trimmed, cut in half
    lengthwise, and well washed
2 tablespoons unsalted butter
Coarse salt to taste
1/3 cup heavy cream
1/4 cup soft goat's milk cheese (usually sold as
    logs in vacuum-packed plastic), rind removed
    if necessary, and broken into pea-size pieces
2 tablespoons chopped flat-leaf parsley leaves
1 1/2 tablespoons chopped tarragon leaves
Freshly ground black pepper to taste
4 slices crusty bread, toasted in the oven
1 clove garlic, peeled

Slice the leeks crosswise to make 1/4-inch half-moons. Melt the butter in a large sauté pan over medium heat. Add the leeks to the pan, season lightly with salt, and cook over low heat until the leeks become meltingly soft but do not color, 8 to 10 minutes. Turn the heat up to high to cook off the excess liquid, 1 to 2 minutes. Reduce the heat to medium-low and pour in the cream. Cook until thickened, about 1 minute. Add the goat's milk cheese and stir for a minute or two until melted slightly but still a bit lumpy. Add the parsley and tarragon and season with salt and pepper to taste. Remove from the heat but keep warm.

Rub the slices of bread with the garlic clove. Mound the leeks on the toast and serve.

John Schenk's Buffalo Chicken Wings

~

MAKES 32 CHICKEN WINGS

When chef John Schenk, executive chef-owner of Clementine restaurant in New York's Greenwich Village, prepared a Superbowl menu on a shoestring, he brought a professional chef's palate to a menu of guilty pleasures like these chicken wings. Highly addictive, they've become the most popular item dispatched by Clementine's sister operation, the Kumquat delivery service. Be sure to use a high-quality hot sauce rather than Tabasco, which will be too spicy and one-dimensional.

If you like, serve these wings with cool, creamy blue cheese dressing (perhaps the one on page 62), which will take the edge off the heat of the sauce and give the palate some relief between bites.

32 large chicken wings
5 tablespoons unsalted butter, melted
3½ tablespoons hot sauce, ideally Frank's

Preheat the oven to 425° F.

Place the chicken wings on a baking sheet and bake for 50 to 60 minutes.

While the wings are cooking, combine the melted butter and hot sauce in a bowl large enough to contain the chicken wings.

Remove the wings from the oven and toss them in the sauce until evenly and well coated. Serve immediately.

John Schenk's Clementine Cheese Fondue with Toasted Baguette

1 baguette, cut into 1-inch cubes
1 tablespoon cornstarch
1 tablespoon cold water
½ cup dry white wine
1 tablespoon unsalted butter
8 ounces Emmentaler cheese, freshly grated (if unavailable, substitute Comté or double the amount of Gruyère)
8 ounces Gruyère cheese, freshly grated

SERVES 2 TO 6

Part of the timeless allure of a fondue is the *caquelon*, the shallow pot in which it is traditionally heated and served. But you need not possess any special equipment to make a creamy and satisfying fondue, as John Schenk proves with this recipe—a late-night favorite on the bar menu in his restaurant, Clementine. Here, the fondue is cooked on the stovetop and transferred to an attractive bowl for presentation. As you'll see, the fondue doesn't suffer at all when prepared in this fashion.

Preheat the oven to 400° F.

Place the baguette cubes on a sheet pan and toast in the preheated oven until golden brown, 5 to 6 minutes. Remove from the oven and reserve.

Using a whisk, mix the cornstarch with the cold water until a thick paste is formed.

In a small stainless-steel or cast-iron saucepan, heat the wine over medium-high heat until warm. Stir in the butter and bring to a simmer. Lower the heat and slowly add the grated cheeses, stirring constantly, until combined. Fold in the cornstarch paste. Remove from the heat, transfer to a fondue pot or other serving vessel, and serve immediately with the toasted bread cubes alongside.

Don Pintabona's Prosciutto-Wrapped Figs with Smoked Mozzarella

SERVES 4 AS AN APPETIZER; 4 WRAPPED FIG PIECES EACH

In this dish, which the Tribeca Grill's executive chef, Don Pintabona, prepared for us on an outdoor grill, the sweet and salty combination of figs and prosciutto is elevated by the presence of mint and smoked mozzarella. Though it's the most expensive variety, seek out prosciutto di Parma for its superior soft texture.

16 fresh mint leaves
8 fresh figs, halved, tough stems discarded
8 ounces smoked mozzarella, cut into 16 ⅛-inch-thick squares
16 very thin slices prosciutto di Parma (about 4 ounces)
2 tablespoons olive oil

Special equipment: 4 6-inch wooden skewers

Lay 1 mint leaf on each fig half. Top each mint leaf with a square of smoked mozzarella. Wrap each fig individually with a slice of prosciutto. Thread 4 wrapped fig halves onto each skewer.

Pour the olive oil into a large nonstick skillet and warm it over moderate heat. Add the fig skewers to the pan and cook until just warm and the prosciutto is slightly crispy, about 1½ minutes. Turn the skewers and cook the other side. Remove from the heat and serve immediately.

Don Pintabona's Caramelized Onion, Gorgonzola, and Rosemary Pizza

SERVES 4

Don Pintabona cooked this rich, creamy, and herbaceous pizza for us in the bona fide pizza oven in his backyard. If you've never made pizza, you may be surprised at how easy it is, even if you don't have an "official" oven. If making pizza at home intrigues you, Pintabona recommends that you invest in a ceramic pizza stone that will fit on the rack in your oven and provide a surface that approximates a professional one.

DOUGH YOUR OWN WAY

If you're wary of making your own pizza dough, many pizzerias will be happy to sell you some.

FOR THE DOUGH:
2 1/4-ounce packages active dry yeast (2 tablespoons total)
1 3/4 cups lukewarm water (105 to 115° F)
6 cups all-purpose flour, plus more for working
1 to 2 teaspoons coarse salt
Olive oil, for the bowl

FOR THE TOPPING:
1/2 cup extra-virgin olive oil
1 tablespoon unsalted butter
4 yellow onions, thinly sliced
2 tablespoons fresh rosemary leaves
Coarse salt and freshly ground black pepper to taste
1/4 cup crumbled Gorgonzola cheese

TO MAKE THE DOUGH (2 12-INCH CRUSTS):

In a large bowl, sprinkle the yeast over the lukewarm water and let stand until dissolved and foamy, about 10 minutes. Add the flour to the bowl, salt to taste, and using your fingers, mix until the water is fully absorbed. Continue to work the mixture with your hands until it comes together.

Transfer the dough to a floured surface and knead until smooth and elastic, about 10 minutes. Shape the dough into a ball and place in an oiled bowl. Cover tightly with plastic wrap and let rise at room temperature in a warm spot until the dough has doubled in size, about 1 hour.

PREPARE THE TOPPING:
Warm the oil and butter in a sauté pan over low heat. Add the onions and rosemary and cook until the onions are soft and translucent, about 30 – 40 minutes. Stir often and add more oil or water if necessary to prevent scorching. Season with salt and pepper and spread out on a sheet pan to cool.

TO SHAPE THE DOUGH:
Transfer the risen dough to a floured work surface. Pound it down and cut it in half. Gently press it out, lifting and stretching it as you work it into 2 rounds about 12 inches in diameter and about ¼ inch thick. Using your fingertips, form a slight rim around the perimeter of each round.

Preheat the oven to 400° F.

Transfer the rounds to floured baking sheets or pizza stones. Let rise in a draft-free place for about 20 minutes.

TO MAKE THE PIZZA:
Spread the onion mixture and scatter Gorgonzola on top of each round. Bake until the top is lightly golden and the crust is browned, about 20 minutes. Cut into wedges and serve immediately.

Erica Miller's Tuna Carpaccio

SERVES 4 AS AN APPETIZER

Classically, carpaccio is a dish of very thinly sliced raw beef dressed with olive oil and topped with mixed greens. But American chefs have used the format of carpaccio to explore other possibilities, most often seafood, a logical extension of the increased popularity of sushi over the past two decades. Here, chef Erica Miller presents her version of tuna carpaccio. While using superior raw ingredients is always essential, the quality of the tuna is paramount here; be sure to seek out the best possible sushi-grade tuna with a bright, ruby red color and be sure that it's well chilled before making the dish.

If you would like to break free of the shoestring realm, top each serving of this carpaccio with ¼ to ½ ounce osetra caviar.

5 to 6 ounces sushi-grade tuna, well chilled

Coarse salt and freshly ground pepper to taste

Olive oil, for brushing

1 medium red onion, cut into ¼-inch dice

½ red bell pepper, seeded and cut into ¼-inch dice

1 cucumber, peeled, seeded, and cut into ¼-inch dice

1 teaspoon extra-virgin olive oil

1 teaspoon white wine vinegar or champagne vinegar

Slice the tuna into 4 equal portions and season with salt and pepper. Place each piece of tuna between 2 pieces of plastic wrap and gently pound them flat to a thickness of ⅛ inch with a meat tenderizer. (If you don't have a meat tenderizer, use the bottom of a heavy pan.) Discard the plastic wrap and place each piece of tuna in the center of a chilled salad plate. Brush the top of the tuna with olive oil and lightly season again.

Mix the onion, red pepper, and cucumber in a small bowl. Drizzle with 1 teaspoon olive oil and the vinegar and season with salt and pepper. Place equal portions of the mixture on top of each tuna slice and serve immediately.

Richard Sandoval's Mahi Mahi Ceviche

SERVES 4

In a ceviche, an acidic marinade (usually made from fresh limes) "cooks" the raw fish. In this recipe, Richard Sandoval makes a traditional ceviche based on the ones he encountered in Guerrero, Mexico, where he spent some time early in his career. Sandoval finds the charm of this recipe rests in its balance—the tartness of the limes, the spiciness of the peppers, and the sweetness of the onion and honey. This last ingredient is the most interesting one; notice how this chef uses honey to adjust the sweetness of the finished dish.

Many recipes instruct you to remove the seeds from jalapeño peppers, but Sandoval invites you to leave them in, as he does at Maya restaurant, and enjoy the full force of their heat. If you prefer a less spicy dish, by all means remove all or some of the seeds.

12 ounces mahi mahi, well chilled
Juice of 8 limes
3 plum tomatoes, seeded and cut into 1/8-inch
    dice
1 jalapeño pepper, finely chopped
½ onion, finely chopped
¾ cup roughly chopped cilantro leaves
Coarse salt and freshly ground black pepper to
    taste
2 tablespoons honey, or to taste

Working on an impeccably clean surface, cut the mahi mahi into ½-inch cubes. Drizzle the cubes with the lime juice, cover, and marinate in the refrigerator, for 1½ hours.

Combine the tomatoes, jalapeño, onion, and cilantro with the mahi mahi and refrigerate for 15 minutes. Season with salt, pepper, and honey to taste. Serve immediately.

Richard Krause's Grilled Mozzarella and Tomato

SERVES 4

It would be difficult to conceive of a less fussy starter than the Italian triumvirate of sliced fresh tomatoes, medallions of mozzarella, and fragrant basil leaves. Drizzled with nothing more than a high-quality olive oil and a few drops of balsamic vinegar, and seasoned with coarse salt and a few grinds of black pepper, this tried-and-true combination remains a fixture on Italian restaurant menus even in these experimental times.

A perfect forum for appreciating fresh tomatoes at the peak of their late-summer season, this salad does, alas, have a limitation the rest of the year, when tomatoes are out of season. Chef Richard Krause, of New York City's Martini's restaurant, devised the following recipe to expand the enjoyment of tomatoes, mozzarella, and basil into a year-round proposition. Krause grills the tomatoes to intensify their flavor. He also quickly cooks the supporting ingredients, including balsamic vinegar and chopped basil, in a simple sauce. The flavors are not only boosted, but the entire dish is warmed, making it a perfect fall-to-winter version of a timeless trio.

FOR THE SKEWERS:
1 2-pound ball fresh mozzarella
8 ¾-inch-thick French bread rounds
4 plum tomatoes, cut in half through the stem
    end
8 fresh basil leaves
¼ cup extra-virgin olive oil (approximately)
Coarse salt and freshly ground black pepper to
    taste

SPECIAL EQUIPMENT:
4 10-inch bamboo skewers

FOR THE SAUCE:
9 plum tomatoes, peeled, seeded, and roughly
    chopped
8 fresh basil leaves, roughly chopped
¼ cup extra-virgin olive oil
Several drops of balsamic vinegar
Coarse salt and freshly ground black pepper to
    taste

PREPARE THE SKEWERS:
Cut the mozzarella in half and then into eight ¾-inch slices. Place the ingredients on the skewers in the following order: bread, tomato, basil, mozzarella, tomato, basil, mozzarella, and bread. Set aside while you make the sauce.

PREPARE THE SAUCE:
Mix all the ingredients together and warm them in a saucepan for 1 to 2 minutes before serving. (You do not want the tomatoes to break down but rather just to be warmed.)

GRILL THE SKEWERS:
Brush the skewered mozzarella and tomato with a little olive oil and season with salt and pepper.

Quickly cook on a flat grill or in a large sauté pan over high heat on both sides until the bread is lightly toasted and the cheese begins to melt, about 30 – 45 seconds per side.

Spoon the sauce onto 4 warm dinner plates. Set the skewers neatly on top of the sauce, slide out the skewers, and serve.

Mario Batali's Marinated Roasted Peppers with Goat Cheese, Olives, and Fett'unta

SERVES 4

This antipasto-style dish is a paean to Mario Batali's love of the contrast between sweet peppers and tangy goat cheese. The olives are much more than a garnish; their saltiness brings a focus and cohesion to the other flavors. Batali explains that his inspiration for this recipe hails from southern Italy, where tomatoes and mozzarella are often combined with salty anchovies or olives. *Fett'unta* is Italian for "oily slice" and refers to toast drizzled with olive oil.

3 large bell peppers, red, yellow, or a combination
8 tablespoons extra-virgin olive oil
12 large green Sicilian olives (these do not need to be pitted)
1 tablespoon balsamic vinegar
$1/4$ teaspoon crumbled dried rosemary
1 8-ounce log fresh goat's milk cheese, cut into 8 $1/2$-inch rounds
8 1-inch-thick slices Italian bread
2 cloves garlic, peeled

Preheat the broiler or grill.

Coat the whole peppers with 2 tablespoons of the olive oil. Place the peppers under the broiler or on the grill and roast, turning often, to blacken the skin evenly all over, 8 to 10 minutes total. Allow to cool, then peel under cold running water, rubbing the skins gently to remove all charred bits. Cut the peppers in half and remove the seeds and stems. Cut into 1-inch-thick strips and place them in a mixing bowl.

Add the olives, vinegar, rosemary, and 2 tablespoons oil to the peppers and toss to mix well. Divide evenly among 4 plates. Place 2 goat cheese rounds in the center of each pepper pile.

Toast the bread until light brown on both sides. Lightly rub the toasts with the garlic cloves and drizzle each piece with ½ tablespoon olive oil. Place the toasts on the plates and serve.

Jeanette Maier's Stuffed Portobello Mushrooms

SERVES 4

This recipe, which executive chef Jeanette Maier serves at her Herban Kitchen restaurant in Greenwich Village, takes full advantage of the generous diameter of a portobello mushroom. When shopping for portobellos, be sure that the mushrooms do not have any white fungus, which will show up first on the stem. Use the firmest mushrooms you can find.

¹/₄ cup soy sauce
2 tablespoons plus 1 teaspoon olive oil
4 large portobello mushrooms, stems trimmed
  and roughly chopped, whole caps reserved
¹/₄ cup finely chopped onion
1 clove garlic, finely chopped
¹/₂ teaspoon dried oregano
Pinch of sea salt
Freshly ground black pepper to taste
3 tablespoons dried bread crumbs

Preheat the broiler.

Mix the soy sauce and 2 tablespoons olive oil together in a small bowl. Dip both sides of the mushroom caps into this mixture to coat, then place them, open side up, on a baking sheet. Place the baking sheet on the center rack of the oven and broil for 15 minutes.

After the mushroom caps have been cooking for 10 minutes, warm the remaining 1 teaspoon olive oil in a sauté pan or skillet over moderate heat. Add the mushroom stems, onion, garlic, oregano, salt, and a splash of water (to keep them from sticking). Season with pepper and sauté for 3 minutes, stirring to combine.

Remove the mushroom caps from the oven and spoon the stem mixture into the caps. Top with the bread crumbs. Return to the broiler for 1 minute to warm and unify the flavors. Remove from the oven, transfer to a serving platter, and serve immediately.

Peter Kelly's Roasted Onions with Bacon and Apple Stuffing

SERVES 4

This is a smoky-flavored fall dish that chef Peter Kelly, of Restaurant X in Congers, New York, usually serves with sweetbreads and foie gras. But here, with just bacon and apples, the strength of the foundation ingredients shines though. Kelly advises home cooks to seek out large fresh onions that aren't soft and to use Cortland or Macintosh apples for their flavor and ability to stand up to high temperatures. Peel and dice the apples as close to preparation time as possible so they won't turn brown.

4 large onions (preferably Walla Walla or Vidalia)

Coarse salt and freshly ground black pepper to taste

1 teaspoon unsalted butter, melted

2 tablespoons balsamic vinegar

8 ounces bacon, cut into small dice

1 tablespoon unsalted butter, at room temperature

2 Cortland or Macintosh apples, peeled, cored, and diced

1½ cups cubed white bread (½-inch dice)

1 tablespoon minced sage leaves (optional)

Preheat the oven to 400° F.

Trim the onion bottoms, so that the onions are able to sit flat without falling over. Cut the tops off the onions, ½ inch from the top. Place the tops back on the onions from which they were sliced and secure with tooth-picks. Place the onions in a roasting pan, sea-son with salt and pepper, and drizzle with the melted butter and vinegar.

Place the onions in the preheated oven and roast until they are soft, about 1 hour. Remove from the oven and set aside to cool.

Remove the tops from the onions and scoop out their centers, being careful not to break the outer layer. Roughly chop the cooked onion centers and set aside.

In a sauté pan large enough to hold all of the ingredients, sauté the bacon in 1 tablespoon butter until well browned, then add the minced onions, apples, bread, and sage. Stir gently and cook for 1 minute just to combine the flavors. Season with salt and pepper and remove from the heat.

Spoon the stuffing into the onions and replace the tops. Return to the oven and bake until the onions are heated through, about 20 minutes. Serve immediately.

Thomas Salamunovich's Smoked Salmon with Crisp Onion Rings, Grilled Asparagus, and Pea Shoots

SERVES 4

Colorado chef Thomas Salamunovich created this irreverent recipe just for "Chef on a Shoestring." As you will see, it turns the onion ring into the base of a light, crunchy salad. Don't skip the step of roasting the whole onion, because this makes it surprisingly sweet. You will need a deep-frying thermometer to make this dish. The oil should measure approximately 2 inches in a small, deep saucepan.

1 large Spanish onion
1 tablespoon olive oil (approximately)
Oil for deep-frying
$\frac{1}{2}$ cup all-purpose flour (approximate)
Tempura Batter (recipe follows)
1 cup pea shoots or thinly sliced arugula
20 English sweet peas, shucked and blanched
12 ounces large asparagus, peeled and grilled
8 tablespoons Red Wine Vinaigrette (recipe follows)
Coarse salt and freshly ground black pepper to taste
2 ounces smoked salmon, cut into 4 thin slices
Juice from 4 Roma tomatoes or $\frac{1}{4}$ cup V8 juice

Preheat the oven to 350° F.

Cut the onion in half horizontally, brush the halves with olive oil, and place face down in a shallow roasting pan. Roast in the preheated oven until golden brown around the edges, about 30 minutes. Remove from the oven and let cool slightly.

Bring a pot of oil for deep-frying to a temperature of 340° F.

Separate the onion halves into individual rounds and select the 4 largest rounds. Lightly dust the rounds with flour, then coat with the tempura batter. Deep-fry in the hot oil until golden brown. Remove with tongs or a slotted spoon, drain on paper towels, and place I round in the center of each of 4 salad plates.

In a clean mixing bowl, toss together the pea shoots, peas, and asparagus. Dress with 6 tablespoons of the vinaigrette and season with salt and pepper. Place one-fourth of the pea mixture in the center of a salmon slice, lining up the asparagus so that they are parallel to the short end of the salmon, and roll the salmon tightly around the greens. Place the salmon roll in the center of one of the onion rings. Repeat this process with the remaining pea mixture, salmon, and onion rings. Sprinkle any remaining peas around each plate. Whisk the tomato juice into the remaining vinaigrette and spoon it around each plate.

Red Wine Vinaigrette

3 tablespoons red wine vinegar
Pinch of sugar
1 clove garlic, minced
Coarse salt and freshly ground black pepper to
    taste
5 tablespoons extra-virgin olive oil

In a small bowl, mix together the vinegar, sugar, and garlic and season with salt and pepper. Gradually whisk in the olive oil.

Tempura Batter

Make this batter in advance (the day before, if you like) and chill it until ready to use.

2 cups all-purpose flour
2³/₄ cups water
2 tablespoons baking powder

Whisk all the ingredients together in a bowl.

Alfred Portale's Creamy Polenta with Cremini Mushrooms

SERVES 4

In this dish, Alfred Portale, the executive chef of the Gotham Bar and Grill, makes polenta—the Italian cornmeal pudding—into a complex component in its own right by first infusing its cooking liquid with garlic and then stirring sautéed mushrooms into the polenta itself. This recipe, a perfect fall starter, also makes an ideal accompaniment to roast chicken and meats.

Mushrooms

2 tablespoons unsalted butter
1 small onion, minced
1 small clove garlic, crushed
1 pound fresh cremini mushrooms, trimmed and
    wiped clean with a damp cloth or paper
    towel
2 tablespoons chicken stock
Coarse salt and freshly ground black pepper to
    taste

In a 12-inch sauté pan, warm the butter over medium heat. Add the onion and cook until softened, about 3 minutes. Add the garlic and cook for 1 minute. Add the mushrooms, cover, and cook until the mushrooms are tender and release their juices, 7 to 10 minutes. If the mushrooms seem dry, add the chicken stock. Season with salt and pepper. Set aside.

Polenta

2 cups milk
1 cup heavy cream
1 cup chicken stock
1 large clove garlic, peeled and crushed under a
    knife
1 cup quick-cooking polenta
Coarse salt and freshly ground black pepper to
    taste

Place the milk, cream, stock, and garlic in a medium saucepan and bring to a simmer over medium heat, being careful not to let it boil over. Remove from the heat and let stand for 10 minutes. Pick out the garlic. Return the liquid to a slow boil and gradually whisk in the polenta. Cook over low heat, whisking constantly, until thick, about 5 minutes. Season with salt and pepper.

Mix about one-third of the cooked mushrooms into the polenta. Divide the polenta evenly among 4 warmed deep soup bowls. Spoon the remaining mushrooms over the polenta. Serve immediately.

Sara Moulton's Quiche Lorraine

SERVES 4

This classic quiche Lorraine, with bacon and Swiss cheese, makes a good starter or small meal in its own right. The recipe may be adapted to include any number of vegetables and meats. To help gain an appreciation of its versatility, think of it as you would an omelet.

Sara Moulton, who hosts a show on the Food Network and is the executive chef of *Gourmet* magazine, recommends pairing the quiche with a salad for an enticing combination of heavy and light sensations. It also makes wonderful cold leftovers. Purchase thick-cut bacon when making this recipe; it's easier to work with.

Flour to lightly cover work surface

Pastry Dough (recipe follows), or 1/4 pound
  frozen puff pastry sheets, thawed

6 thick slices bacon, cut crosswise into 1/2-inch
  pieces

2 large eggs plus 2 large egg yolks, at room
  temperature

1 1/2 cups heavy cream

2 teaspoons Dijon mustard

1/2 teaspoon coarse salt

Pinch of freshly grated nutmeg

Freshly ground black pepper to taste

3/4 cup grated Wisconsin Swiss cheese

Preheat the oven to 375° F.

On a lightly floured surface using a rolling pin dusted with flour, roll out the dough to a uniform thickness of 1/8 inch and work it into a 12-inch round. Fit the dough into a 9-inch tart pan with a removable bottom. Prick the bottom of the shell in several places with a fork and refrigerate for 30 minutes until firm.

Meanwhile, in a heavy 8- to 10-inch skillet, cook the bacon over moderate heat until lightly browned and crisp, about 5 minutes. Remove it from the skillet with a slotted spoon or tongs and allow to drain on paper towels. Using a whisk or electric beater, combine the eggs, cream, mustard, salt, and nutmeg. Season with black pepper and stir in the cheese.

Remove the pastry shell from the refrigerator and place the pan on a baking sheet. Scatter the bacon over the bottom of the tart shell, then gently ladle the egg mixture over the top, making sure to leave an inch of tart shell visible. Bake in the upper third of the oven for 25 minutes until the custard has puffed and browned and a toothpick inserted in the center comes out clean. Remove from the oven and allow to cool slightly.

To remove the quiche from the pan, set the pan on a large jar or coffee can and slip down the outside rim. Run a long metal spatula under the quiche to make sure it isn't stuck to the bottom of the tin, then slide the quiche onto a heated platter. Cut into quarters and serve warm or at room temperature.

Pastry Dough

(adapted from Gourmet magazine)

The amount of water necessary to make pastry dough changes slightly from time to time, depending on variables such as humidity and the moisture content of the butter and flour.

1 1/4 cups all-purpose flour

6 tablespoons (3/4 stick) unsalted butter, chilled,
  cut into 1/2-inch cubes

2 tablespoons vegetable shortening, chilled

1/4 teaspoon coarse salt

2 to 4 tablespoons ice water

TO BLEND BY HAND:

In a bowl with your fingertips or a pastry blender, blend together the flour, butter, shortening, and salt until most of the mixture takes on the appearance of a coarse meal with the remainder in small, roughly pea-size lumps. Drizzle 2 tablespoons of the ice water evenly over the mixture and gently mix with a fork until incorporated. Test the mixture by gently squeezing a small handful. It has attained the proper texture when it holds together without crumbling. If necessary, add some of the remaining water, I tablespoon at a time, stirring until incorporated and testing for the proper texture. Be very careful not to overwork the mixture or add too much water or the pastry will be tough.

To blend in a food processor:

In the food processor, pulse together the flour, butter, shortening, and salt until most of the mixture resembles coarse meal with the remainder in small, roughly pea-size lumps. Add 2 tablespoons ice water and pulse 2 or 3 times, just until incorporated. Test the mix-

ture by gently squeezing a small handful. It has attained the proper texture when it holds together without crumbling. If necessary, add some of the remaining water, I tablespoon at a time, pulse 2 or 3 times after each addition until incorporated, and test for the proper texture. Be very careful not to overprocess the mixture or add too much water or the pastry will be tough.

To form the dough after blending:

Turn the dough out onto a work surface and divide into 4 equal portions. With the heel of your hand, smear each portion once in a forward motion to help distribute the fat. Gather the dough together and form it, rotating it on the work surface, into a disk. Chill the dough, wrapped in plastic wrap, until firm, at least I hour or for as long as I day. This recipe makes enough dough for a single-crust 9-inch pie or an I I-inch tart.

Salads

Erik Blauberg's Baby Arugula Greens with Watermelon "Croutons" and Caesar Dressing

SERVES 4

This crowd-pleasing summer starter from '21' Club chef Erik Blauberg finds chilled, sugary cubes of watermelon complemented by peppery arugula and dressed with a tangy Caesar dressing. This well-chosen composition of sensations allows the diner to experience a full range of flavors, from the sweet, refreshing watermelon to the creamy dressing. And the bright colors, reminiscent of a Matisse canvas, perfectly reflect the season for which this recipe was designed.

½ loaf Italian bread or baguette
1 teaspoon minced shallot
6 ounces arugula, stems removed, washed and dried
Erik Blauberg's Caesar Dressing (recipe follows)
Freshly ground pepper to taste
8 ounces watermelon, seedless or seeds removed, cut into ½-inch cubes (1¾ cups)

Preheat the oven to 350° F.

Cut the bread into 1-inch cubes and place on a sheet pan. Sprinkle the shallot on top and toast in the preheated oven until golden brown and crunchy, about 5 minutes. Remove from the oven.

In a mixing bowl, toss the arugula, warm bread, and dressing. Season with pepper. Divide this salad among 4 salad plates, then artfully stack equal portions of the watermelon on top. Serve immediately.

Erik Blauberg's
Caesar Dressing

～

MAKES ABOUT 1 CUP

To create the famous '21' Caesar dressing, add 1 tablespoon beluga caviar or North Carolina trout roe to the dressing just before seasoning with salt and pepper.

1 large egg yolk, at room temperature
1 teaspoon Dijon mustard
Juice of 1 lemon
1 anchovy fillet, chopped (optional)
½ cup extra-virgin olive oil
1 cup freshly grated Parmesan cheese
2 tablespoons roughly chopped flat-leaf parsley
    leaves
Coarse salt and freshly ground black pepper to
    taste

Pour the egg yolk into a wooden mixing bowl and whisk in the mustard. Add the lemon juice and continue to whisk. If using the anchovy, add it now and whisk well.

While whisking, add the olive oil in a thin stream until it is fully incorporated and the mixture is emulsified.

Whisk in the grated cheese and add the parsley.

Season to taste with salt and pepper and refrigerate until ready to use.

NOTE: Raw eggs carry the risk of salmonella, and recipes containing them should not be served to the very young, the very old, pregnant women, or anyone with a compromised immune system.

John Schenk's Classic Caesar Salad

SERVES 4

If you prefer a more conventional Caesar salad—or a dressing that doesn't call for a raw egg.

2 teaspoons anchovy purée, about 6 fillets

1 large or 2 medium cloves garlic, minced

¾ teaspoon dry mustard

1 teaspoon Worcestershire sauce

2 tablespoons fresh lemon juice

½ cup extra-virgin olive oil

Coarse salt and freshly ground black pepper to taste

3 heads romaine lettuce, outer leaves removed, remaining leaves separated, washed, dried, and cut into small pieces

¾ cup (approximately 3 ounces) grated Parmesan cheese

In a nonreactive salad bowl, mash the anchovies and garlic together with a fork. Add the dry mustard and Worcestershire and mix well. In a separate mixing bowl, using a whisk, incorporate the oil gradually into the lemon juice until an emulsion forms, then whisk this emulsion into the anchovy mixture until fully incorporated. Season with salt and pepper.

Toss the romaine with the dressing, adding the grated Parmesan a third at time. If necessary, adjust the seasoning. Serve immediately.

Aaron Bashy's Braised Leek Salad

SERVES 4

This recipe unlocks the full flavor potential of the leek by caramelizing it in a warm pan. Be very careful to cook the leeks just enough to soften them but try to keep them al dente, or firm to the bite. Even if it doesn't scorch, overcooking the leek will drain it of its sweet flavor, so get it out of the pan as soon as it's warmed through.

2 large leeks, thick green tops trimmed and discarded, root ends trimmed but intact, cut in half lengthwise, and well washed in cold water
1 tablespoon extra-virgin olive oil
Splash dry white wine, such as Chardonnay (optional)
2 tablespoons red wine vinegar
2 tablespoons chicken stock or water
Coarse salt and freshly ground pepper to taste
4 tablespoons crumbled feta cheese
3 tablespoons finely diced Kalamata olives, from about 10 whole olives

Thoroughly dry the leeks. Warm the olive oil in a sauté pan set over moderate heat. Add the leeks to the pan, flat side down. Caramelize the leeks, paying close attention to doing so without burning or scorching the delicate vegetable, about 4 minutes. Remove the leeks from the pan using tongs or a slotted spoon.

If using wine, deglaze the pan with it and cook until the wine is reduced by half, a few seconds. Add the vinegar to the pan and reduce by one-third, another few seconds. Add the chicken stock and reduce by half, again, just a few seconds.

Place 1 leek half on each of 4 salad plates. Season with salt and pepper. Check the pan sauce for seasoning and adjust if necessary. Drizzle equal portions of the sauce over the leeks, sprinkle with the crumbled cheese, and garnish with the olives.

Walter Staib's Cucumber and Cream Salad

(adapted from The City Tavern Cookbook*)*

⁓

SERVES 4

Walter Staib delights in recreating recipes from "America's first gourmet restaurant." "Generations ago," says Staib, "this salad would only be served in the warmer months, when cucumbers were in season." Though today you could, of course, prepare it at any time of year, it's still best enjoyed in the spring, when the cold, crunchy cucumbers provide welcome relief after months of root vegetables. Even if you aren't a fan of spicy food, don't leave out the cayenne pepper; it adds a crucial bit of heat to the recipe.

1 large English cucumber or 2 medium cucumbers, peeled and thinly sliced into rounds
Coarse salt
1/2 cup sour cream
1 tablespoon white wine vinegar
Pinch cayenne pepper
2 pinches ground paprika
1/2 onion, finely chopped
Coarse salt and freshly ground white pepper to taste
6 to 8 fresh chive leaves, finely chopped

Place the cucumbers in a mixing bowl, sprinkle with salt, cover, and refrigerate for 1 hour to render out the moisture.

Remove the cucumbers from the refrigerator, place in a colander, and rinse thoroughly but gingerly with softly running cold water. Gently squeeze out all excess water by pressing on the cucumber slices with a rubber spatula.

In a small mixing bowl, combine the sour cream, vinegar, cayenne, paprika, and onion. Add this mixture to the cucumbers, toss to combine, and season with salt and pepper. Garnish with the chives and serve.

Bill Wavrin's Spinach and Red Onion Salad

(adapted from the Rancho La Puerta Cookbook)

SERVES 4

Bill Wavrin is the executive chef of Rancho La Puerta, a world-renowned spa in Baja California. At the spa's own Tres Estrellas (Three Stars) ranch, they grow great quantities of spinach when it's in season and—in an effort to use as much of it as possible—Wavrin has created a number of recipes that employ the leafy green. This colorful and swiftly prepared salad is one of the chef's favorites from his own repertoire. One of its most appealing attributes is that the vibrant colors—red onion, green spinach, and orange zest—are an accurate reflection of the distinct flavors within. Other ingredients that contribute important contrasts are the bitter radicchio and the chopped egg whites. If you don't care for cilantro, feel free to leave it out.

½ red onion, thinly sliced
1 teaspoon fresh lime juice
⅓ cup fresh orange or grapefruit juice
¼ cup red wine vinegar
1 shallot, minced
2 cloves garlic, minced (if you love garlic, go ahead and add another clove)
1 tablespoon chopped orange zest
½ teaspoon roughly chopped basil leaves
½ teaspoon roughly chopped cilantro leaves
½ teaspoon roughly chopped oregano leaves
¼ teaspoon roughly chopped thyme leaves
Freshly ground black pepper to taste
3 quarts spinach leaves (about 1½ pounds)
1 head radicchio, separated into leaves
2 large hard-cooked egg whites, roughly chopped
1 carrot, grated
6 sprigs basil (optional)

In a small bowl, toss the onion and lime juice and set aside for a few minutes to soften the onion's "edge."

In another small bowl, combine the orange juice, vinegar, shallot, garlic, orange zest, and chopped herbs. Season with pepper.

Put the spinach and radicchio in a large bowl and add the egg whites, carrot, and marinated onion. Drizzle with the vinaigrette and toss well. Serve on chilled plates and garnish with herb sprigs if desired.

Ira Freehof's Hearts of Lettuce with Blue Cheese Dressing

SERVES 4

"Years ago, when you ordered a salad with blue cheese dressing, the waitress would always groan 'fifty cents extra'," says Ira Freehof, the proprietor of two Comfort Diners in New York City and someone who does a more than passable impression of a beleaguered diner waitress. In this recipe, a little blue cheese goes a long way, so much so that it even meets our shoestring criteria. To reinforce the dish's retro roots, Freehof turns to iceberg lettuce, which has been all but abandoned by contemporary restaurant chefs. Note also that he doesn't emulsify the dressing but merely stirs its ingredients together to allow the rich texture of the cheese to make an impact in the final dish.

1 head iceberg lettuce, washed, dried, cored, and cut into quarters
1 large ripe beefsteak tomato, cored and cut into 8 wedges
12 black olives, pitted
Ira Freehof's Blue Cheese Dressing (recipe follows)

Arrange the lettuce wedges along with the tomatoes and olives on salad plates. Drizzle with the blue cheese dressing.

Ira Freehof's
Blue Cheese Dressing

~~~

MAKES ABOUT 1¼
CUPS

4 ounces crumbled blue cheese, such as
    Roquefort or Gorgonzola
3 tablespoons milk
½ cup mayonnaise
6 tablespoons extra-virgin olive oil
¼ cup dry white wine
1 teaspoon Dijon mustard
Pinch of coarse salt
Pinch of freshly ground black pepper

In a small bowl, mash the blue cheese and milk with a fork until creamy. Add the rest of the ingredients and whisk until well mixed. Cover and refrigerate until ready to use.

John Villa's Boston
Lettuce Salad with
Green Beans and
Lemongrass Dressing

~~~

SERVES 4

This crunchy green salad was part of a Thai-inspired menu that John Villa, the chef of Pico restaurant in New York City, prepared for us one summer morning. Be sure to buy the freshest green beans and lettuce you can find. If you have a hard time locating lemongrass, substitute the grated zest of 1 lemon; it won't have the same distinctive flavor but will approximate the acidity crucial to the balance of the dressing.

Coarse salt to taste
20 green beans, trimmed
1 teaspoon sugar
1 clove garlic, peeled
1/2 stalk fresh lemongrass, roughly chopped
1 shallot, thinly sliced
1 green Thai chili, or jalapeño pepper, seeded
    and roughly chopped
2 tablespoons rice vinegar
2 tablespoons extra-virgin olive oil
1 head Boston lettuce, separated into leaves,
    washed, and dried
Freshly ground black pepper to taste

Bring a pot of lightly salted water to a boil and prepare an ice water bath (page 227) in a bowl large enough to contain the beans. Blanch the green beans in the boiling water for just 1 minute. Remove the beans from the water and "shock" them in the ice water to stop the cooking and preserve the beans' color. Remove the beans from the ice water and drain.

Grind the sugar, garlic, lemongrass, shallot, and chili using a mortar and pestle or the bowl of a ladle until a homogenous paste is formed. Transfer to a mixing bowl and whisk in the vinegar and oil. Toss this mixture with the lettuce leaves and green beans. Season with salt and pepper and serve immediately.

Nick Stellino's Mushroom Salad

SERVES 4

One-fourth cup olive oil to sauté the mushrooms may seem excessive, but PBS culinary personality Nick Stellino says the generous quantity serves a purpose: "The mushrooms soak up the flavorful oil and then give it off after they're cooked."

1/4 cup extra-virgin olive oil
1 1/2 pounds cremini mushrooms, trimmed,
    wiped clean with a damp cloth or paper
    towel, and cut into 1/4-inch dice
1/4 teaspoon coarse salt, plus more to taste
1/8 teaspoon freshly ground black pepper, plus
    more to taste
1/8 teaspoon hot red pepper flakes
4 cloves garlic, roughly chopped
1 1/2 tablespoons roughly chopped flat-leaf
    parsley leaves
1/2 cup white wine

In a large nonstick sauté pan, heat the olive oil over high heat until it is almost smoking. Add the mushrooms and cook for 2 minutes without stirring. Stir and cook for 1 additional minute.

Marcus Samuelsson's Asparagus and Bean Sprout Salad with Dill Pesto

Add the salt, black pepper, red pepper flakes, garlic, and parsley. Cook for 2 minutes, stirring continuously. Add the white wine and cook until the liquid is almost entirely evaporated, about 3 minutes. Taste and adjust the seasoning. Serve immediately.

SERVES 4

The Italian condiment pesto was created to celebrate the distinct flavors of Genoese basil, a superb and delicate herb that's significantly more aromatic and flavorful than domestic varieties. Contemporary American chefs have created their own versions of pesto using a variety of herbs and varying the supporting ingredients as well.

In this recipe, Aquavit chef Marcus Samuelsson—perhaps the premier Swedish chef in the United States—substitutes that most beloved Swedish herb, dill, for basil in this variation of the Italian classic. In the spirit of thrift, Samuelsson incorporates mixed salted nuts, instead of pine nuts, a most uncommon ingredient from a three-star chef. In the late summer, you may substitute white asparagus, but this expensive option will definitely take you out of the shoestring realm.

Coarse salt

1/2 pound large green asparagus, peeled ("large" applies to average-size stalks, as opposed to "jumbo" or "colossal")

1 bunch (25–30 sprigs) fresh dill, large stems removed

1 cup mixed salted nuts

2 tablespoons freshly grated Parmesan cheese

1 cup extra-virgin olive oil

Freshly ground black pepper to taste

2 cups bean sprouts

Prepare an ice water bath in a bowl large enough to contain the asparagus. (See page 227.)

Bring a medium-size pot of salted water to a boil. Add the asparagus to the boiling water and cook for 4 minutes. Remove the asparagus from the water using tongs or a slotted spoon and "shock" the asparagus in the ice bath to stop the cooking process and preserve its verdant color. Remove the asparagus from the ice bath, allow to dry on paper towels, cut into ½-inch pieces, and set aside.

Place the dill, nuts, and Parmesan in a food processor and pulse until smooth. With the machine running, slowly drizzle the olive oil into the mixture in a steady stream until emulsified but with a slightly grainy consistency. Season with salt and pepper to taste.

Toss the asparagus and sprouts in a large bowl with all but 4 tablespoons of the dill pesto and place an equal portion in the center of each of 4 salad plates. Spoon a small amount of pesto around the perimeter of each plate and serve immediately.

Michael Romano's Warm Shrimp and Bean Salad with Arugula

SERVES 4

In this warm salad, Michael Romano of New York City's Union Square Café coaxes as much flavor as possible out of the ingredients by sautéing them together. The shrimp are warmed and gently crisped before precooked white beans are added to the same pan, allowing their flavors to meld. The cool bed of arugula provides subtle contrasts of flavor, texture, and temperature.

If your budget permits, Romano suggests that you might add more shrimp or use the more luxurious lobster. You might also make this dish the base of a seafood salad by adding mussels, clams, and/or calamari.

4 cups arugula, stemmed, washed, dried, and
 torn into 1-inch pieces

¼ cup extra-virgin olive oil, plus 1 tablespoon
 for drizzling

2 teaspoons minced garlic

16 medium shrimp (about 4 ounces), shelled,
 deveined, and butterflied

1½ cups cooked cannellini or Great Northern
 beans, plus ¼ cup of their cooking liquid

1 tablespoon minced basil leaves

Coarse salt and freshly ground black pepper to
 taste

2 teaspoons fresh lemon juice

Arrange the arugula on a serving platter or in a large salad bowl. Set aside.

Warm ¼ cup olive oil and the garlic in a 10-inch skillet over moderate heat for 1 minute, being careful not to brown the garlic. Add the shrimp to the pan and cook until they turn pink and lose their raw appearance, 2 to 3 minutes. Add the cooked beans and cooking liquid to the pan, raise the heat, and bring to a boil. Lower the heat and cook until the liquid is almost completely evaporated, 3 to 4 minutes. Stir in the basil and season with salt, pepper, and lemon juice.

Spoon the warm shrimp and beans on top of the arugula. Drizzle with 1 tablespoon olive oil and serve immediately.

Kerry Heffernan's Roasted Root Vegetable Salad

SERVES 4

This salad is a perfect restorative way to begin a cold-weather meal. Roasting the carrots, parsnips, and beets softens them and deepens their distinct individual flavors while unifying their textures. Don't depend on the cooking time in the recipe when roasting; since the water content of the vegetables may vary dramatically, keep a close eye on each of them to be sure they don't overcook and dry out.

To approximate the version of this dish that Heffernan serves at Eleven Madison Park, top the plated vegetables with 1 slice of goat's milk cheese before you reheat them in the microwave.

FOR THE SALAD:

2 large or 3 medium carrots, cleaned and
    trimmed

2 large or 3 medium parsnips, cleaned and
    trimmed

2 large or 3 medium beets, cleaned and trimmed

Coarse salt and freshly ground black pepper to
    taste

6 tablespoons grape seed oil or canola oil

1 bunch watercress, washed and dried

¼ pound mixed salad greens, washed and dried

FOR THE DRESSING:

1 large egg yolk, at room temperature

2 tablespoons red wine vinegar

2 tablespoons water

1 teaspoon dried mustard or 1 tablespoon Dijon
    mustard

Coarse salt and freshly ground black pepper to
    taste

1 teaspoon marjoram leaves

1 teaspoon roughly chopped flat-leaf parsley

6 tablespoons grape seed oil or canola oil

Preheat the oven to 350° F.

Place the carrots, parsnips, and beets in 3 separate small roasting pans, one type in each. Season each vegetable with salt and pepper and drizzle with grape seed oil. Place ¼ to ½ cup water in the bottom of each pan and cover each pan with aluminum foil. (The water is to keep the vegetables from drying out; determine the amount of water by how dry the vegetables are.) Place the pans in the preheated oven, ideally on the same rack, and roast for 30 minutes.

After 30 minutes, remove the parsnips from the oven and keep covered to retain the heat. Remove the foil from the carrots but continue cooking them for 10 to 15 additional minutes. Also remove the foil from the beets and let them cook for about another 30 minutes. Roast until the vegetables are gilded and a sharp, thin-bladed knife can be easily inserted into them.

While the vegetables are cooking, make the dressing: Place the egg yolk, vinegar, water, and mustard in a blender and season with salt and pepper. Blend for 30 to 45 seconds, starting at low speed and gradually increasing to high. When the dressing becomes frothy, add the herbs, then begin to drizzle in the oil in a thin stream until well blended.

When the vegetables are done, remove them from the oven, peel, and slice thin on a diagonal. Arrange the vegetables, alternating colors, on 4 salad plates. (If necessary, reheat in the microwave for 15 to 20 seconds at this point.) Place a small bouquet of watercress and mixed salad greens on each plate with the vegetables.

Sprinkle the dressing over the salad greens and vegetables and serve.

NOTE: Raw eggs carry the risk of salmonella, and recipes containing them should not be served to the very young, the very old, pregnant women, or anyone with a compromised immune system.

Walter Staib's Curried French Lentil Salad and Sausage

(*adapted from* The City Tavern Cookbook)

⌁

SERVES 4

This salad from City Tavern chef Walter Staib combines sausage, French lentils, and a complex dressing for a sophisticated dish that, in the days of the original City Tavern, would only be encountered in an upscale colonial restaurant. The recipe illustrates how American chefs of that day emulated French and Continental styles, but made resourceful use of ingredients to which they had easy access, such as dried beans.

FOR THE LENTILS:

2 cups dried French green lentils

1 tablespoon extra-virgin olive oil

½ yellow onion, finely chopped

1 clove garlic, very finely chopped

1 bay leaf

1 teaspoon dried thyme leaves

1 teaspoon curry powder

Coarse salt and freshly ground black pepper to taste

8 ounces cooked pork sausage

2 teaspoons unsalted butter

2 carrots, cut into extra-fine julienne

2 plum tomatoes, peeled, seeded, and cut into julienne

FOR THE DRESSING:

3 pinches cayenne pepper

1 tablespoon Dijon mustard

1 teaspoon curry powder

¼ cup extra-virgin olive oil

3 tablespoons red wine vinegar

6 to 8 fresh chive leaves, finely chopped

3 cloves garlic, finely chopped

½ onion, finely chopped

Coarse salt and freshly ground black pepper to taste

Rinse the lentils in several changes of cold water. Place in a small bowl and cover with cold water. Cover the bowl with a lid or plastic wrap and refrigerate the beans overnight. Drain well.

In a medium-size stockpot, warm the olive oil over moderate heat. Add the onion and garlic and cook until translucent, 4 to 5 minutes, stirring occasionally to avoid scorching. Add the lentils, bay leaf, thyme, and curry powder and season with salt and pepper. Cook for an additional 3 minutes. Add enough water to cover the contents of the pot, raise the heat to high, and bring the water to a boil. Lower the heat until the liquid is just simmering, cover, and cook until the lentils are cooked through, 15 to 20 minutes. (Check frequently by simply squeezing or tasting one.) Drain the lentils and discard the bay leaf.

Place the sausage and butter in a skillet and cook slowly over low heat until the sausage is heated through, about 5 minutes for precooked sausage and 10 minutes for fresh. Remove the sausage from the skillet to a plate covered with paper towels to absorb the grease. Transfer the sausage to a clean, dry cutting board, cut into fine julienne, and set aside.

In a separate bowl, prepare the dressing by combining all of the ingredients except the salt and pepper. Stir well to combine, then season to taste with salt and pepper. Add the lentils, carrots, tomatoes, and sausage to the dressing. Gently toss, adjust the seasoning if necessary, and serve.

Terrance Brennan's Roasted Beet Salad with Arugula and Aged Goat Cheese

SERVES 4

Picholine restaurant is known for having one of the most remarkable cheese selections in New York City. Appropriately enough, on two occasions, Picholine's executive chef, Terrance Brennan, visited our show and demonstrated how to make salads featuring cheese as the first course of his shoestring meal. This one uses aged goat cheese, which is a bit creamier and more pungent on the palate than the fresh version.

2 medium beets

7 tablespoons extra-virgin olive oil

½ cup red wine vinegar

1 medium shallot, finely chopped (1 tablespoon)

Coarse salt and freshly ground black pepper to taste

1 large bunch arugula, tough stems trimmed and discarded, washed and dried

2 ounces aged goat's milk cheese, at room temperature, crumbled

¼ cup walnuts, chopped and lightly toasted (optional)

Special equipment: mandoline (optional, but very useful for slicing the beets)

Preheat the oven to 375° F.

Place the beets on a 12- x 12-inch sheet of aluminum foil and coat with 2 tablespoons of the olive oil. Bring the edges of the aluminum foil together to cover the beets in a loose package. Place the beets in their foil package in a roasting pan and bake for approximately 45 minutes until a thin-bladed knife or skewer slides easily into the beets. (It's okay to pierce right through the foil when performing this test.) Remove the beets from the foil and set aside to cool.

When the beets are cool enough to handle, peel them; their skins should slip right off at this point. Slice them as thin as possible, preferably with a mandoline.

Pour the vinegar into a small stainless-steel bowl and whisk in the remaining 5 tablespoons olive oil. Add the shallot and season to taste with salt and pepper.

Transfer 1 tablespoon of the vinaigrette to a small bowl. Divide the beet slices evenly among four 10-inch plates, slightly overlapping them and covering the bottom of each plate. Using a pastry brush, lightly coat the beets with the 1 tablespoon vinaigrette.

Toss the arugula with the remaining vinaigrette and distribute evenly among the 4 plates, piling the arugula neatly on top of the beets.

Distribute the crumbled goat cheese, and the walnuts if using them, on top of the arugula. Serve immediately.

Terrance Brennan's Pear and Gorgonzola Salad

SERVES 4

In this salad from Picholine chef Terrance Brennan the succulent sweetness of pears contrasts with the creamy richness of Gorgonzola cheese. Rather than using mesclun greens, Brennan plays this combination against the slightly bitter flavor of crisp watercress.

2 ripe Bartlett pears
1 lemon (optional)
¼ cup extra-virgin olive oil
3 tablespoons balsamic vinegar
Coarse salt and freshly ground black pepper to taste

8 ounces Gorgonzola or goat's milk cheese, at room temperature, cut into 4 same-shape wedges
2 bunches watercress, tough stems trimmed and discarded, washed and dried
16 walnut halves, coarsely chopped and lightly toasted

Cut the pears in half and remove the cores and stems with a melon baller. Cut off a thin slice of the round part of each pear half so it will sit flat on a plate. Set aside. (If not serving immediately, rub all cut surfaces of the pears with lemon juice to keep them from oxidizing and turning brown.)

Whisk the olive oil into the vinegar. Season with salt and freshly cracked black pepper.

Set a pear half in the center of each salad plate. Lean 1 cheese wedge against each pear half or stack it on top of the pear. Drizzle a total of 2 tablespoons of the vinaigrette evenly over the pears. Toss the watercress with the remaining vinaigrette and mound it on top of the pears, being careful not to topple the cheese. Sprinkle with the walnut pieces and season with salt and freshly cracked black pepper to taste.

Soups and Stews

Jim Coleman's Chicken Pot Pie

(*adapted from* The Rittenhouse Hotel Cookbook)

SERVES 4

In this unusually constructed pot pie, chef Jim Coleman of Philadelphia's five-diamond–rated Rittenhouse Hotel cooks squares of dough in the broth itself rather than baking a crust over the pie—an approach modeled after the one favored by the Amish in nearby Lancaster, Pennsylvania. Coleman explains that he was preparing a pot pie for a special event when his sous chef, who grew up near Lancaster, insisted that a true "pot pie" is made in an actual pot, and what most Americans consider "chicken pot pie" should rightfully be called "chicken pie."

You may add your favorite seasonal vegetables to this pot pie, but avoid fibrous ones such as asparagus or broccoli, which will break down when cooked. In the fall and winter months, root vegetables, such as turnips, parsnips, or rutabaga, make especially good additions.

2 quarts chicken broth or water
2 8-ounce skinless, boneless chicken breasts, cut into 1½-inch pieces
2 medium Idaho russet potatoes, peeled and cut into 1-inch chunks
1 medium onion, cut into ¼-inch dice
2 carrots, peeled and cut into ¼-inch dice
2 celery stalks, cut into ¼-inch dice
1 tablespoon chopped fresh garlic
Pinch of saffron
¼ cup roughly chopped flat-leaf parsley leaves
¼ teaspoon chopped fresh thyme leaves
¼ teaspoon chopped fresh rosemary leaves
Jim Coleman's Pot Pie Squares (recipe follows)
Coarse salt and freshly ground black pepper to taste

Bring the broth to a boil in a large stockpot and add the chicken, potatoes, onion, carrots, celery, garlic, and saffron. Lower the heat and cook at a gentle simmer for about 15 minutes. Add the herbs and the pot pie squares and cook until the dough is tender, about 20 minutes. Because the potatoes will take the longest to cook through, check for doneness by inserting a sharp, thin-bladed knife into one of the pieces of potato in the pot. As soon as the knife slides in and out easily, remove the pot from the heat.

Season the soup with salt and pepper. Ladle into individual bowls and serve piping hot.

Jim Coleman's Pot Pie Squares

MAKES APPROXI-
MATELY 30 SQUARES

These pot pie squares expand to twice their uncooked size when placed in simmering water or stock. They were designed for the chicken pot pie on page 75 but may be used to add extra taste and substance to almost any soup.

1 cup all-purpose flour, plus more for dusting the work surface
1/4 teaspoon coarse salt
1/4 teaspoon dried thyme
1 teaspoon finely chopped flat-leaf parsley leaves
1 large egg, at room temperature
3 1/2 tablespoons milk

Combine the flour, salt, thyme, and parsley in a bowl. Add the egg and milk and work them together to form a soft dough. Be careful not to overwork the dough or it will become tough.

On a lightly floured surface, roll the dough out to the thickness of a nickel. Cut into 2 x 1-inch rectangles.

John Doherty's Fresh Pea Soup with Brook Trout Goujonettes and Parsley Salad

SERVES 4

Chef John Doherty of New York's fabled Waldorf-Astoria hotel insists that this soup be made only with fresh peas that are young and sweet, which makes it a May/June proposition only. Keep a close eye on the soup when cooking, because overheating will turn it an unattractive brown color. If it comes out thicker than you like it, strain it for a smoother consistency. The brook trout *goujonettes* make this a more substantial soup.

3 cups light chicken stock or water

Coarse salt to taste

2 pounds fresh pea pods, shucked, pods
    reserved (1½ cups shelled fresh peas)

2½ tablespoons unsalted butter

½ onion, cut into ¼-inch dice

Freshly ground black pepper to taste

2 tablespoons extra-virgin olive oil

Juice of 1 lemon, or to taste

Trout Goujonettes (recipe follows)

Parsley Salad (recipe follows)

Bring 3 cups of salted water to a boil, add the peas, and cook for 1 minute. Drain the peas, reserving the water, and place the peas in an ice water bath to "shock" them, stopping the cooking and preserving their beautiful green color. Drain and set aside.

In a 2-quart saucepan, melt 1 tablespoon of the butter over moderate heat, add the onion, and gently cook until translucent, 3 to 4 minutes. Add the empty pods and the reserved pea cooking liquid. Season with salt and pepper. Simmer for 2 minutes. Strain the liquid, discard the pods, and pour the liquid into a blender. Add the cooked peas and purée until smooth. (You may need to work in batches, adding a third of the liquid and a third of the cooked peas at a time.) Add 1 tablespoon butter, the olive oil, and lemon juice to the blender and purée. Taste and adjust the seasonings and acidity if necessary and blend again. (If necessary, gently rewarm soup before serving.)

Arrange the trout and parsley in the middle of 4 large soup bowls. Grind some black

pepper over the fish and bring to the table. Ladle the soup around the trout at the table.

Trout Goujonettes

2 cups cooking oil

1 fresh whole brook trout or 12 ounces trout
    fillet, skin and bones removed (ask your
    fishmonger to do this)

Coarse salt and freshly ground black pepper to
    taste

1 cup all-purpose flour

1 large egg, beaten

1 cup dried bread crumbs or cornmeal

Heat the oil in a deep saucepot to 325° F. Cut the fish fillets into thin strips approximately ½ inch wide. Season the strips with salt and pepper. Coat each strip first with flour, then dip in the egg and then into the bread crumbs. Carefully lower several strips at a time into the oil and fry until golden brown. Using tongs or a slotted spoon, remove from the oil and drain on paper towels. Repeat with the remaining strips.

Parsley Salad

½ bunch flat-leaf parsley
1 teaspoon extra-virgin olive oil
Coarse salt and freshly ground black pepper to
taste

Pick and clean the smallest parsley leaves. Coat with the olive oil and season with salt and pepper.

Rick Moonen's Gazpacho

SERVES 4

While the gazpacho Rick Moonen serves at Oceana restaurant might have an island of crabmeat or lobster piled high in the center of the bowl, here he focuses instead on extracting the maximum flavor from each vegetable and herb—tomato, garlic, peppers, and cilantro. Following the classic model, he also adds a healthy dose of vinegar to up the acidity, creating a potent, cocktail-like concoction.

To ensure the proper cool temperature in the bowl, Moonen tosses some ice cubes into the mixture before grinding. "The ice melts," he explains, "but the salt in the recipe draws out enough flavorful juices from each ingredient to form little pools of flavor."

Moonen's recipe diverges from the traditional Spanish varieties in one other way—no bread. As a nod to convention, Moonen suggests serving his version with grilled peasant bread drizzled with olive oil on the side.

½ cup ice cubes, plus enough for an ice water
   bath
½ yellow onion, cut into large chunks
2 cucumbers, peeled, seeded, and cut into large
   chunks
1 red bell pepper, seeded and cut into large
   chunks
½ jalapeño pepper, seeded and roughly chopped
½ cup fresh cilantro leaves, plus more for
   garnish
4 scallions, top 2 inches and root ends trimmed
   and discarded
3 large ripe beefsteak tomatoes, seeded and
   halved
1 clove garlic, peeled and finely chopped
⅓ cup ketchup
⅓ cup red wine vinegar
1 teaspoon Tabasco sauce
Coarse salt and freshly ground black pepper to
   taste

Prepare an ice water bath (see page 227).

Place the onion, three-fourths of the cucumber, the bell pepper, jalapeño, cilantro, scallions, tomatoes, garlic, and ½ cup ice cubes in the work bowl of a food processor. Pulse the vegetables until diced, being careful not to overprocess and liquefy.

Transfer the vegetables to a mixing bowl and add the ketchup, vinegar, and Tabasco. Season to taste with salt and pepper and place the mixing bowl in the ice bath to cool the gazpacho. Once the gazpacho is chilled, cover it and refrigerate until it is very cold. Taste and adjust the flavor: add more salt, pepper, and/or Tabasco until the gazpacho is to your taste. Add cold water if the gazpacho is too thick.

When ready to serve, divide the soup among 4 bowls and garnish with the remaining diced cucumber and cilantro.

Roe Di Bona and Sue Torres' Chilled Avocado and Grapefruit Soup with Chipotle Chile Purée

SERVES 4

Roe Di Bona, owner of the Rocking Horse Café Mexicano in New York City's thriving Chelsea neighborhood, began experimenting with the combination of grapefruit and avocado several years ago. She found the two ingredients to be an ideal pairing: the acid of the grapefruit cuts the buttery richness of the avocado pulp. The Rocking Horse began serving avocado and grapefruit tequila drinks and then an ice cream made from the same ingredients. It wasn't long before she and former Rocking Horse chef Sue Torres created this stunning chilled soup.

¼ cup vegetable oil
1 leek, well washed and chopped into 1-inch pieces
1 clove garlic, minced
1 celery stalk, cut into 2-inch pieces
1 medium Idaho or russet potato, peeled and cut into large chunks (optional for thickening)
Sea salt to taste
6 cups vegetable stock or water
2 ripe Hass avocados
1 grapefruit, sectioned, individual sections peeled, juice reserved
Juice of 1 lime
Chipotle Chile Purée (recipe follows)

Warm the vegetable oil in a saucepan over medium heat. Add the leeks and sauté until translucent. Add the garlic to the pan and cook until golden brown, 3 to 5 minutes. Add the celery, potato if using, and a light sprinkle of salt. Cook for 5 minutes. Add the vegetable stock, raise the heat to high, and bring to a boil. Lower the heat and simmer until the liquid is reduced to half the original volume, about 35 minutes. Remove from the heat and set aside to cool to room temperature.

Peel and pit the avocados. Purée the cooled liquid in a blender jar with the avocados, grapefruit segments and juice, and lime juice. Season to taste with salt. Serve chilled with the chipotle purée spooned on top.

"The only avocados I recommend using in Mexican cuisine are called Hass," says Di Bona. "Dark green, slightly weird-looking, and bumpy, Hass avocados can look like something out of science fiction, which makes sense because when perfectly ripe, their flavor is out of this world!" Di Bona advises that when shopping for avocados you seek out those that give just a little when pressed. If you can't find any that meet this description, you may ripen rock-hard avocados by placing them in a bowl and storing them somewhere warmer than room temperature. This takes up to 3 days, so be sure to plan ahead.

Roe Di Bona and Sue Torres' Chipotle Chile Purée

"At the Rocking Horse, we add chipotle purée to give the avocado and grapefruit soup a smoky, spicy flavor," says Di Bona. "If it is added judiciously, you will ensure that the subtle flavor of the avocados and citrus is not overwhelmed by the chili's piquant smack."

2 chipotle chilies (see box, next page)
1 small roasted tomato (see instructions on next page)
Sea salt to taste

Purée all ingredients in a blender jar until roughly blended. Set aside.

CHIPOTLE CHILIES

Di Bona offers the following chipotle wisdom: "The chipotle variety is one of the more widely known chilies from the central state of Oaxaca. They are smoked ripened jalapeños sold dried or canned in adobo (a marinade). If you are using dried chilies, remove the stems (seeds and veins as well, if you prefer a milder sauce). Toast the chilies in a sauté pan until slightly darkened and the aroma wafts from the pan, 1 to 2 minutes on each side. Place the toasted chilies in a non-reactive bowl and cover with boiling water. Let the chilies steep for about 20 minutes until softened, then drain and discard the water. Chipotles sold in adobo are easier to use; they are canned and ready to go."

ROASTING TOMATOES

Preheat oven to 200° F. Slice tomato thinly and coat both sides with olive oil (about ½ tablespoon total). Season both sides with salt and pepper. Spread slices on a sheet pan and roast in oven for about 20 to 25 minutes. Gently flip with a spatula and roast an additional 4 to 5 minutes. Remove from heat.

Pilar Sanchez's Potato and Garlic Soup

SERVES 4

Pilar Sanchez, formerly the executive chef of The Restaurant at Meadowood in California's Napa Valley, was inspired by our $20 challenge to return to the one-pot cooking of her childhood. This very simple recipe creates a satisfying and flavorful soup with relatively few ingredients. Season this dish carefully, being sure to draw out as much of the potato flavor as possible without overseasoning.

2 tablespoons canola oil

½ onion, cut into ¼-inch dice

6 to 8 cloves garlic (about ½ bulb), roughly chopped

2 pounds Idaho or russet potatoes, peeled and roughly chopped

2 quarts vegetable or chicken stock

1 8-ounce can tomato sauce

Coarse salt and freshly ground black pepper to taste

Croutons, for garnish

4 sprigs flat-leaf parsley, stems discarded, roughly chopped

In a large heavy-bottomed soup pot, warm the oil over moderate heat. Add the onion and sauté for 2 minutes. Add the garlic to the pot and cook for 2 minutes, stirring occasionally. Add the potatoes and stock to the pot, raise the heat to high, and bring to a boil. Lower the heat and simmer until the potatoes are very tender and break apart with a fork, about 20 minutes.

Add the tomato sauce to the pot, raise the heat to high, and return to a boil. Remove the pot from the heat and purée the soup in small batches in a blender or food processor. Return the soup to the pot and place it over low heat to rewarm it, 2 to 4 minutes. Season to taste with salt and pepper. Ladle into individual bowls and garnish with croutons and parsley.

Mike Smith's Corn and Potato Chowder

~

SERVES 4

Mike Smith, who was the executive chef of New York City's Blackbird restaurant when he appeared on our show, makes a few adjustments to this New England–style chowder in order to meet the increasing American demand for low-fat and vegetarian cooking. Traditionally, a chowder is made with salt pork and finished with cream or milk, but here, Smith omits both. At the restaurant, he used a vegetable stock made with corn husks to infuse the stock with extra flavor and reinforce the corn theme of the dish. Home cooks should feel free to do the same or simply substitute chicken stock for the water.

While this vegetable soup is satisfying, Smith is quick to add that when he makes it for himself at home, "I definitely add some cream."

Like many soups, this one may be prepared a day in advance and reheated.

2 tablespoons unsalted butter
2 small Spanish onions, cut into 1/4-inch dice
2 cloves garlic, minced
2 tablespoons all-purpose flour
6 cups water
1 teaspoon dried thyme leaves
2 medium Idaho or russet potatoes, peeled and cut into 1/2-inch dice
2 ears fresh corn, husked and cut in half crosswise
Coarse salt and freshly ground black pepper to taste
3 scallions, thinly sliced

In a small pot, melt the butter over low heat. Add the onions and garlic and gently sauté until softened, 3 to 4 minutes, being careful not to allow either to color. Add the flour, stir well to coat the garlic and onions, and cook for about 2 minutes until the flour has absorbed the butter. Slowly stir in the water. Raise the heat to high, bring to a boil, and add the thyme, potatoes, and corn. Lower the heat and simmer until the liquid has thickened slightly, about 25 minutes. Remove the corn from the pot and let it cool for 2 minutes. When cool enough to handle, shave the corn off the cobs and add the kernels to the pot. Season with salt and pepper, garnish with the scallions, and serve.

Richard Vellante's Caldo Verde

SERVES 4

Richard Vellante, the vice president of Food Operations and executive chef of Massachusetts-based Legal Sea Foods restaurants, bases his *caldo verde* on the Portuguese soup, which is made with potatoes, kale, and chorizo. (The word *verde* means "green" and refers to the seaweed tint of the kale.) Here, Vellante adds littleneck clams and mussels, whose briny quality, he feels, has a great affinity with chorizo. This recipe is an occasional special at Legal Sea Foods restaurants, usually in the winter, when its hearty qualities are most welcome. Feel free to vary the seafood to suit your own taste.

1 pound Idaho or russ[et]
    cut into ½-inch-thi[ck]
3 cups water
8 tablespoons extra-[virgin olive oil]
1 teaspoon coarse s[alt]
2 cloves garlic, peel[ed]
½ teaspoon hot red pepper flakes
4 sprigs thyme
1 pound linguiça or chorizo sausage, sliced ¼ inch thick
8 littleneck clams, scrubbed
1 pound mussels, scrubbed and debearded (see page 127)
½ cup dry white wine
¼ pound kale, well washed and thinly sliced
Freshly ground black pepper

Place the potatoes in a large soup pot with the water and 1 tablespoon of the olive oil. Add 1 teaspoon salt, the garlic, pepper flakes, and thyme sprigs to the pot and bring to a boil over high heat. Lower the heat to bring the soup down to a simmer. Simmer, stirring occasionally with a whisk to break up the potatoes, until the potatoes are completely dissolved and the broth is shiny and lightly thickened, about 35 minutes. Remove and discard the thyme sprigs.

Meanwhile, place 1 tablespoon of the olive oil in a 2- to 3-quart saucepan and warm it over moderate heat. Add the sausage to the pan and brown it all over, about 2 minutes. Add the shellfish and white wine to the pan. Cover and steam until the shellfish open, about 4 minutes. Discard any shellfish that did not open. Transfer the remaining shell-age, and liquid to the pot with the ring potato broth.

Add the kale to the soup and simmer for 2 more minutes. Season with salt and pepper, ladle soup into individual bowls, and serve at once.

Eric Ripert's Onion Soup

SERVES 4

In this rustic dish, intended as a companion recipe to his stuffed tomatoes (page 33), chef Eric Ripert employs a classic country presentation that has great taste benefits, using the onion itself as a "bowl" for the soup. "The sweetness of the raw onion contrasts very well with the cooked vegetable in the soup," explains the chef.

In true shoestring fashion, Ripert chose to make this soup with Italian pecorino Romano cheese, rather than the conventional French Gruyère, because the former was on sale the day he shopped for the show. Feel free to use either, but if you opt for pecorino Romano, be especially careful not to overseason the soup; much of the cheese's saltiness will be imparted to the broth.

4 large Spanish onions
4 ounces (1 stick) unsalted butter
2 tablespoons all-purpose flour
1 14½-ounce can chicken broth
Sea salt and freshly ground white pepper to
taste
1 cup half-and-half
¼ cup grated pecorino Romano or Gruyère
cheese

Do not peel the onions. Trim the root ends so that they are flat enough for the onions to stand up, because they will be used as the "bowl" for this soup. Cut a ¾-inch-thick "lid" from the top of each onion and set aside. Using an ice cream scoop or spoon, carefully scoop out the inside of the onions, leaving at least 2 outer layers; they should each be thick enough to hold the soup.

Roughly chop the onion scraps. Set aside one-fourth of the onion scraps for the stuffed tomato recipe (page 33) or another dish, or else discard.

Preheat the broiler.

Melt the butter in a heavy-bottomed 2-quart saucepan over medium heat. Add the chopped onion and cook until tender, limp, and lightly caramelized, about 15 minutes. Add the flour to the pan, stir to incorporate, and cook for 5 minutes. Add the chicken broth, stir to incorporate, and cook for another 15 minutes. Season with salt and pepper to taste. Add the half-and-half and cook for 10 more minutes.

Place the "onion bowls" on a sheet pan and ladle equal amounts of soup into each onion. Top with the cheese and place under the broiler. Cook until the cheese is bubbly and browned, 2 to 3 minutes. Set the onion "lids" slightly askew on the onions to reveal the gratinéed soup within.

Jane and Michael Stern's Cincinnati Five-Way Chili

(adapted from Chili Nation)

⁓

SERVES 4

This recipe hails from Jane and Michael Stern's book *Chili Nation*, which presents a chili recipe from each of the fifty states. This one, a Cincinnati institution in its own right, is named "five-way" because there are five layers in the classic configuration. The Sterns advise that if you don't have cardamom or coriander on hand, you should substitute your own favorite spices. There's no "official" five-way recipe—each cook has his or her own secret variation—so adjusting it to your personal taste would be a fitting gesture.

1¼ pounds ground beef
2 medium onions, roughly chopped
2 cloves garlic, minced
1 cup favorite barbecue sauce (pick a good one for its flavor will influence this dish)
½ cup water
½ ounce unsweetened chocolate, grated
1 tablespoon chili powder
1 teaspoon freshly ground black pepper
¼ teaspoon ground cumin
¼ teaspoon ground turmeric
¼ teaspoon ground allspice
¼ teaspoon ground cinnamon
¼ teaspoon ground cloves
¼ teaspoon ground coriander
¼ teaspoon ground cardamom
½ teaspoon coarse salt
Tomato juice, as needed
9 ounces dried spaghetti
1 tablespoon unsalted butter
1 16-ounce can red kidney beans
1 pound Cheddar cheese, finely shredded
Oyster crackers, for garnish

In a large skillet or Dutch oven, brown the meat with half the onions and all the garlic, stirring to keep it loose. This should take 6 to 8 minutes. Drain any fat from the pan. Add the barbecue sauce and the water and bring the mixture to a boil. Add the chocolate, spices, and salt. Cover, reduce the heat, and simmer for 30 minutes, stirring occasionally. The chili will thicken as it cooks. Add tomato juice as needed to create a brew that ladles up easily. Allow the chili to rest at least 30 minutes in a covered pan at room temper-

Sara Moulton's Miniature Pumpkin Soup with Ginger and Toasted Pumpkin Seeds

ature. (Chili may be refrigerated and reheated to serve.)

Just before serving, cook the spaghetti in a large pot of boiling salted water until just a bit softer than al dente. Drain and toss with the butter.

Rinse the beans and heat them in a small saucepan over medium heat until warm. Drain any excess liquid.

To make each plate, start with a layer of spaghetti; top it with the hot chili and then a few warm beans and some of the remaining chopped onion. Pat on some cheese so the chili's heat can begin to melt it. Serve immediately with oyster crackers.

For our Halloween show a few years ago, Sara Moulton prepared this beautifully presented soup, a creamy but creamless concoction, served in hollowed-out miniature pumpkin shells. You might think of miniature pumpkins as purely ornamental, but Moulton insists that they are "hands down the best-tasting pumpkin you'll ever eat." You may use regular pumpkin or acorn or butternut squash but, of course, will need to serve it in a regular bowl rather than a pumpkin shell.

8 miniature pumpkins

2 teaspoons vegetable oil, plus more for the
   baking sheets

Coarse salt to taste

1½ tablespoons unsalted butter

1 cup thinly sliced onion (1 medium onion)

1 tablespoon freshly grated ginger

3 cups water, plus additional to thin if necessary

Freshly ground black pepper to taste

Preheat the oven to 350° F.

Remove the stem end from 4 of the pumpkins, cutting about one-fourth of the way down from the top. Wipe the lids clean with a paper towel and reserve. Remove the strings and seeds from the pumpkins, taking care not to cut into the flesh, and discard.

Cut the 4 remaining pumpkins in half horizontally and remove the strings and seeds, again being careful to avoid cutting into the flesh. Reserve the seeds from 2 of the pumpkins and discard the remaining seeds and strings. Wash the reserved seeds, pat dry with paper towels, and set aside.

Lightly oil 2 baking sheets. Place all of the pumpkins, cut side down, on the baking sheets. Bake in the preheated oven for 40 minutes until they are tender. Remove from the oven and set aside to cool. When the pumpkins are cool enough to handle, remove the flesh from the pumpkin halves by scraping them out and discarding the shells. Also remove most of the flesh from the remaining 4 pumpkins but leave enough inside to help them retain their shape because they will be used as soup bowls.

Reduce the oven temperature to 250° F.

In a small mixing bowl, toss the reserved seeds with 2 teaspoons oil and season with salt. Spread the seeds out in a single layer on a baking sheet. Bake on the center rack of the oven, stirring occasionally, for 1 to 1½ hours until they are golden and crisp. Remove the baking sheet from the oven and set aside to allow the seeds to cool.

Place the butter in a medium skillet and warm over moderate heat. Reduce the heat to low and add the onion and the ginger to the skillet. Cook, stirring, until the onion is softened and translucent, about 5 minutes. Add the pumpkin flesh and the water to the skillet and simmer for 20 minutes. Remove from the heat.

In a blender, purée the pumpkin mixture in batches and transfer to a saucepan. Season with salt and pepper and add additional water if necessary to thin the soup until it's creamy but not excessively thick. (Feel free to adjust the thickness to your personal taste.) Set aside until ready to serve.

Return the oven temperature to 350° F.

Place the reserved pumpkin shells, cut side up, on a baking sheet and place in the oven on the center rack to warm for 15 minutes. Meanwhile, return the saucepan of soup to the stove and warm over moderate heat.

Carefully remove the pumpkin shells from the oven and arrange on 4 soup plates. Divide the soup evenly among the plates, filling each shell about three-fourths of the way up and ladling the remaining soup around the pumpkin shell into the bowl itself. Sprinkle the seeds over the top and serve with the lids over the pumpkins.

On the Street

The first part of each "Chef on a Shoestring" segment is pre-taped, usually on a Thursday morning. Producer Jee Won Park, the guest chef, and a camera person visit a market in New York City to shop for the ingredients that will be used in the cooking demonstration. These field pieces offer a colorful window into the range of gastronomic oases in Manhattan. They've allowed our viewers to make virtual visits to such famous shopping destinations as the Chelsea Market, Fairway, the Union Square Greenmarket, and, on one rare, extravagant occasion, Dean & DeLuca.

Most chefs will tell you that selecting superior raw ingredients is more than half the battle of great cooking. The chef might explain why he or she is selecting a certain mushroom over another; or the sights and smells that indicate a fresh piece of fish; or what kind of rice they think is best for paella. Every episode of "Chef on a Shoestring" features five or six nuggets of wisdom that our audience can take to the market the next time they go shopping.

As the chefs tick off items on their shopping list, Jee keeps them on their toes with a running tally of the expense on a hand-held calculator. She's also become a bit of an acting coach, working with the camera person to help the chefs squeeze their information into short sound bites and to strike just the right tone—a balance of enthusiasm and wisdom. The shopping segments end just as yours do—with checkout at the register and the moment of truth, whether or not the ingredients come under $20. (Thanks to Jee's constant budgetary updates, they always do.) When they do, we pay for our groceries, and everyone goes his or her own way, with plans to reconvene in the studio on Saturday morning.

—*Hal Gessner*

David Amorelli's White Bean and Sausage Stew

SERVES 4

"I grew up in a house that was half-Italian and half-Irish, so one-pot cooking is part of my family history," says David Amorelli, the executive chef of Cité restaurant in midtown Manhattan. Amorelli enjoys cooking ingredients together to combine the flavors as soon and as completely as possible. Here, the beans absorb some of the sausage's fat as well as its garlic and fennel seasoning. Amorelli recommends this stew for a Sunday dinner. It will fill your home with a powerful and pleasing aroma.

1 pound dry white beans
6 Italian sausages, hot or sweet
1 bay leaf
1½ teaspoons coarse salt, plus more to taste
2 tablespoons extra-virgin olive oil
1 cup finely diced carrots
1 cup finely diced onion
1 cup finely diced celery
3 tablespoons minced garlic
1 cup dry white wine
Freshly ground white pepper to taste

Lay the beans out on a sheet pan. Pick out and discard any broken or discolored pieces. Transfer the beans to a bowl and add enough water to cover. Let the beans soak for 2 hours. Drain the beans and put them in a pot with 3 times as much water as beans. (Note: You may soak the beans in the same pot you plan to cook them in.) Add the sausages and bay leaf to the pot. Place the pot over high heat and bring the liquid to a boil. Reduce the heat to bring the liquid down to a simmer and simmer for 15 minutes. Remove the sausage from the pot using tongs or a slotted spoon and let cool. Continue cooking the beans for 1 hour, until tender. Stir in ½ teaspoon salt, remove the pot from the heat, and let the beans cool in their cooking liquid for 15 to 20 minutes. Drain the beans, being sure to reserve a few cups of the cooking liquid. Purée ½ cup beans and 2 cups of the cooking liquid in a food processor or blender and reserve. Slice the sausages.

Preheat the oven to 325° F.

In a Dutch oven, heat the olive oil to the smoking point over medium-high heat. Add the carrots and onion and sauté until the onion is translucent, about 5 minutes. Add the celery and garlic and cook until you can smell the garlic, about 30 seconds. Add the white wine and cook for 30 seconds. Add the beans, sausages, and bean purée. Season with salt and pepper, cover, and cook in the preheated oven for 35 to 40 minutes.

If you find the stew too thick, add some of the reserved bean cooking liquid to thin it. Serve immediately.

Waldy Malouf's Turkey Noodle Soup

MAKES 1 GALLON

This recipe represents shoestring cooking at its best. It's a great way to use the turkey bones from a Thanksgiving dinner. It comes from Waldy Malouf, executive chef of Beacon restaurant in New York City. Note how the technique allows this recipe to work with the remains of a large or small bird.

1 roasted turkey carcass from an 8- to 14-
    pound bird
1 medium onion, roughly chopped
2 celery stalks, roughly chopped
1 carrot, roughly chopped
1 leek, roughly chopped
Herb Sachet (recipe follows)
4 tablespoons (½ stick) unsalted butter
1 cup finely diced onion
1 cup finely diced celery
1 cup finely diced button mushrooms
¼ cup all-purpose flour
8 ounces egg noodles
2 tablespoons chopped sage leaves
Coarse salt and freshly ground black pepper to
    taste

Cut the turkey carcass in half and place both halves in an 8-quart stockpot. Add enough water to cover the bones by 1 inch. Add the roughly chopped onion, celery, carrot, and leek and the herb sachet to the pot. Place over high heat and bring to a boil. Lower the heat to let the liquid simmer and allow to simmer for 2 hours. Remove from the heat and strain the stock through a colander into a bowl. Let the stock cool briefly. Pick all the meat off the bones and reserve. Do not rinse out the stockpot.

Over moderate heat, melt the butter in the stockpot. Add the finely diced onion, celery, and mushrooms to the pot and sauté until the vegetables soften without coloring, about 4 minutes. Sprinkle the flour over the vegetables, stir to coat, and cook for 1 minute.

Return the strained turkey stock to the stockpot with the cooking vegetables. Raise the heat to high. Bring the liquid to a boil, then lower the heat and allow the soup to simmer for 30 minutes. Add the noodles, reserved turkey meat, and the sage to the pot and simmer for another 10 minutes. Season with salt and pepper and serve immediately.

Herb Sachet

1 tablespoon black peppercorns
1 teaspoon dried thyme
1 bay leaf
4 or 5 sprigs parsley
2 cloves garlic, smashed

Wrap all the ingredients in a sack fashioned from cheesecloth and tie tightly at the top.

Pasta
and
Risotto

Michael Lomonaco's Basic Pasta Dough

MAKES ABOUT 1 POUND PASTA

The notion of making pasta from scratch may strike fear into the hearts of American home cooks, but it's done frequently and nonchalantly in countless households across Italy. This basic recipe freezes very successfully in batches. No salt is used because it toughens the eggs, and the pasta will get all the salt it needs from the water in which it will ultimately be cooked.

This northern Italian–style method of making pasta uses eggs, though you may substitute water if you desire a drier result.

2 large eggs (or ³/₄ cup water approximately)
1¹/₂ cups unbleached all-purpose flour

Special equipment: roller-type pasta machine or rolling pin

On a clean, dry work surface, make a mound of the flour and, using your fingers, make a well in the center of the mound. Break the eggs one by one into the center of the well.

Using a fork, beat the eggs well. Again using the fork, slowly begin to fold the flour in toward the center of the well to incorporate the flour into the beaten eggs. As you mix the flour and the eggs, it will create a doughy mass. Work this mass using your fingers until it begins to lose its moist and sticky character.

When the mass begins to feel uniformly dry, work the dough using both hands: Knead with the palms of both hands, pushing outward from the center of the ball of dough and then folding the near edge inward to begin the kneading cycle again. The kneading stage should take about 10 minutes.

After the dough has been fully kneaded, thin the dough into sheets suitable for cutting: Cut the ball of dough into 3 equal pieces. Form these pieces by hand into equal rectangles to be passed through the rollers of the pasta machine or rolled out with the pin. Set the cylindrical rollers at their widest opening, put a piece of dough in the space between the rollers, and crank the handle to pass the dough through. As each sheet of pasta comes out of the rollers it should be set on a dry cotton towel to rest while you begin rolling the next piece. Thin the dough by rolling each piece through ever thinner settings on the pasta machine, thinning and then setting aside each piece consecutively.

If you do not have a pasta machine, you may roll the pieces out using a rolling pin. Roll them to a thickness of about ⅛ inch, turning the sheets of dough as you roll to ensure a uniform thickness. (Be sure to roll in one direction only—toward you—to help attain this result.)

Mario Batali's Basic Pasta Sauce

MAKES 4 CUPS

This very basic southern Italian sauce may put an end to your expectation of basil in a tomato sauce. There's none here, and none of Mario Batali's Greenwich Village restaurants have suffered for the lack of it. This simple sauce is the glue that holds Batali's kitchens together and, in his largely stock-free cooking, it gets quite a workout.

¼ cup extra-virgin olive oil
1 Spanish onion, cut into ¼-inch dice
4 cloves garlic, thinly sliced
1 tablespoon dried thyme, or 3 tablespoons fresh thyme leaves, chopped
½ medium carrot, finely shredded
2 28-ounce cans peeled whole tomatoes, crushed by hand and juices reserved
Coarse salt to taste

In a 3-quart saucepan, warm the olive oil over medium heat. Add the onion and garlic and cook until soft and light golden brown, 8 to 10 minutes. Add the thyme and carrot and cook until carrot is quite soft, about 5 minutes more. Add the tomatoes with their juices

and bring to a boil, stirring often. Lower the heat and simmer until the sauce is as thick as hot cereal, about 30 minutes. Season with salt and serve.

NOTE: The sauce may be held 1 week in the refrigerator or up to 6 months in the freezer.

Michael Lomonaco's Fresh Homemade Pasta with Wild Mushrooms

SERVES 6 AS AN APPETIZER OR 4 AS A MAIN COURSE

This dish, a sort of open-faced ravioli, tosses a sauce of wild mushrooms with squares of pasta. Feel free to vary the mushrooms, combining your favorites or using just one type, to experience the myriad pleasures of this highly versatile recipe.

For a lighter version of this recipe, simply omit the cream. For a vegetarian option, use vegetable broth in place of the chicken stock. To deepen the flavor, add fresh thyme or tarragon at the end of the cooking, or a few tablespoons of finely sliced sun-dried tomatoes at the same time you add the cream and stock.

Michael Lomonaco's Basic Pasta Dough (page 97)

2 tablespoons extra-virgin olive oil

2 tablespoons finely chopped shallots or onions

1 tablespoon chopped garlic

¼ teaspoon hot red pepper flakes

2 ounces dried porcini mushrooms, washed and rehydrated

8 ounces cremini mushrooms, trimmed, wiped clean with a damp cloth or paper towel, and sliced

Coarse salt and freshly ground black pepper to taste

½ cup heavy cream

½ cup chicken broth

6 to 8 quarts water

1 tablespoon coarse salt

2 tablespoons roughly chopped flat-leaf parsley leaves

¼ cup freshly grated Parmesan cheese

Cut the pasta into 4-inch squares.

In a sauté pan, heat the olive oil over moderate heat. Add the shallots, garlic, and pepper flakes and quickly sauté, being careful to avoid browning or burning. Add the mushrooms, season with salt and pepper, and sauté together for 5 minutes. Add the cream and chicken broth, reduce the heat to prevent the cream from scorching, and cook for several minutes while the pasta cooks.

Bring the water to a rolling boil in a large pot and add the salt. Add the pasta to the boiling water.

Add the parsley and Parmesan to the mushrooms. The pasta should cook for just 1 to 2 minutes after returning to the boil. (Fresh pasta cooks quickly.) When the pasta is done, drain the pasta and toss it with just enough sauce to coat. Spoon servings into large bowls and spoon additional sauce over the top. Serve immediately.

Mario Batali's Ziti al Telefono

SERVES 4

The origin of the Neapolitan dish's name speaks volumes about the creative spirit of Italian cooking. Any dish made with mozzarella cheese carries the suffix *al telefono*, a playful reference to the way the melted cheese strings out from the plate like a curled telephone cord.

6 quarts water (approximately)
2 tablespoons coarse salt
2 cups Mario Batali's Basic Pasta Sauce (page 98)
2 medium tomatoes, cut into ¼-inch cubes
¼ cup basil leaves
1 pound dried ziti
8 ounces fresh mozzarella cheese, cut into ¼-inch cubes

Bring the water to a boil in a large pot and add the salt.

In a 12- to 14-inch sauté pan, combine the pasta sauce and tomato and bring to a boil over high heat. Lower the heat to a simmer and add the basil leaves without stirring.

Meanwhile, cook the pasta according to the package instructions until tender and just shy of al dente, about 10 minutes. (The pasta should be al dente about the same time the basil is added to the tomatoes.) Drain well, then add to the pan with the sauce. Add the mozzarella and toss over medium heat until the cheese is just melting. Pour into warm bowls and serve immediately.

Eric Ripert's Steamed Mussels with Linguine

SERVES 6 AS AN
APPETIZER OR 4 AS
A MAIN COURSE

You won't find this Italian pasta on the menu at Le Bernardin, but it is occasionally presented as a special of the day. At the restaurant, chef Ripert uses a wider tagliatelle noodle instead of linguine, and you should feel free to substitute your own favorite, such as spaghetti or bucatini. Do not use fresh pasta for this dish.

2 tablespoons extra-virgin olive oil

4 cloves garlic, minced

1 onion, very thinly sliced

1 beefsteak tomato, peeled, seeded, and chopped (see page 227)

½ cup white wine

2 pounds mussels, scrubbed and debearded (see page 127)

6 quarts water

Coarse salt to taste

1 pound dried linguine

2 cloves garlic, roughly chopped

2 tablespoons roughly chopped flat-leaf parsley leaves

Freshly ground black pepper to taste

In a large skillet, heat 1 tablespoon of the olive oil over moderate heat. Add the minced garlic, onion, tomato, wine, and mussels to the oil. Cover and let steam until the mussels open, about 5 minutes. Remove the mussels from the broth and cover them to keep them warm. Discard any mussels that do not open and reserve the mussel broth.

Meanwhile, bring the water to a boil in a large pot. Salt the water, add the pasta, and cook until al dente, 8 to 10 minutes. Drain the pasta.

In a large sauté pan, heat the remaining 1 tablespoon olive oil over moderate heat. Add the chopped garlic and 1 tablespoon of the parsley to the oil and season with salt and pepper to taste. Cook until the garlic is translucent, about 3 minutes, and remove from the heat. Add the cooked pasta and toss until thoroughly combined.

Transfer equal portions of the pasta to 4 dinner plates or large bowls. Arrange equal portions of the mussels around each serving of pasta. Spoon the mussel broth from the skillet over the pasta and garnish with the remaining 1 tablespoon parsley.

Alfonso Contrisciani's Sweet Potato Gnocchi

SERVES 6 AS AN APPETIZER OR SIDE DISH

Gnocchi are unique among pasta in that they are made principally of potato rather than flour. This autumnal gnocchi recipe uses deep-orange sweet potato, blending it with white Idaho potato to provide some essential starchiness (which holds the gnocchi together) and the appropriate fluffy texture, and to moderate the intense flavor of the sweet potato.

If you think of gnocchi as dense, leaden lumps, you may not have had one that's properly made. Chef Alfonso Contrisciani, of Atlantic City's Showboat Hotel and Casino, offers a crucial tip for making gnocchi successfully: Cook the potatoes in their jackets, then work with their pulp while it's still hot. This will allow you to form the dumplings before too much moisture has been generated by the heat of the potatoes, which will ensure the proper light and airy consistency.

2 medium or 1 large sweet potato, cooked, peeled, and milled or mashed with a potato masher

1 medium Idaho or russet potato, cooked, peeled, and milled or mashed with a potato masher

2 large egg yolks, at room temperature

3/4 cup all-purpose flour

1/2 cup semolina flour

1 teaspoon ground nutmeg, or to taste

Coarse salt to taste

2 tablespoons unsalted butter, at room temperature

2 tablespoons chopped flat-leaf parsley leaves

FROZEN GNOCCHI

Gnocchi may be frozen in the same manner as ravioli. Place the prepared gnocchi on a sheet pan and allow to harden in the freezer, then transfer to zip-lock bags and freeze for up to 2 months. Frozen gnocchi may be cooked in boiling water without first thawing them, but allow a few extra minutes for cooking.

Combine all the ingredients except for the butter and parsley. Mix thoroughly but gently, with as little friction as possible. You want to avoid developing the gluten in the dough, or the gnocchi will toughen and sink when cooked.

Roll the dough out, cut it into small pieces about 1 inch square, and shape each piece into a small ball, again being careful not to overwork it.

Bring a large pot of salted water to a boil, add the gnocchi, and cook until they float to the top, 2 to 3 minutes. Remove the gnocchi with a slotted spoon and toss with the butter and parsley. Serve immediately.

Bobby Flay's Saffron Risotto with Sautéed Shrimp

"I make my risotto exactly opposite of the way the great Italian chefs do," says Bobby Flay, who adds stock to his rice in three or four large installments, rather than in smaller ladlefuls. The result is a creamier-than-average risotto with a firm al dente core at the center of each grain. And how did Mr. Flay hit upon this technique? "It's called 'I'm-from-New-York-City-and-I-don't-have-time-to-wait,'" he says.

5 cups lobster or shrimp stock
5 tablespoons extra-virgin olive oil
½ medium Spanish onion, cut into ¼-inch dice
3 cloves garlic, finely chopped
2 cups dry white wine
2 cups Arborio rice
1 tablespoon saffron threads
1 tablespoon honey
2 tablespoons coarsely chopped fresh tarragon leaves
Coarse salt and fresh ground black pepper to taste
12 large shrimp, shelled and deveined

Bring the stock to a simmer in a saucepan.

In a large saucepan, heat 3 tablespoons of the oil over medium-high heat. Add the onion and garlic and sweat until soft but not colored, 3 to 4 minutes. Raise the heat to high and add the wine. Cook, stirring constantly, until the wine reduces and the pan is almost dry. Reduce the heat to medium, add the rice and saffron, and stir until the rice is well coated, approximately 2 minutes.

Add 1½ cups of the stock to the rice and cook, stirring continuously, until the liquid is absorbed. Repeat with a second 1½ cups, stirring until the additional stock has been absorbed. Continue to add stock in 1- to 1½-cup increments, cooking and stirring until it is absorbed and the rice is plump but still a bit al dente. Add the honey and the tarragon and season to taste with salt and pepper.

Heat the remaining 2 tablespoons oil in a large sauté pan over high heat. Season the

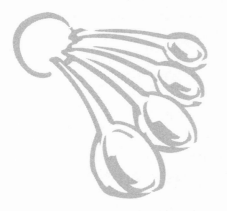

shrimp with salt and pepper to taste. Sauté 2 to 3 minutes on each side.

Spoon the risotto into a large serving bowl. Arrange the shrimp over the risotto and serve immediately.

Nick Stellino's Pasta all'Arrabbiata

SERVES 6 AS AN APPETIZER OR 4 AS A MAIN COURSE

Pasta *all'arrabbiata* is an unusual Italian recipe that is spicy-hot, with the level of heat varying from restaurant to restaurant and chef to chef. "Mine is moderately spicy," says Stellino, "but if you want it hotter, crank up the red pepper. It's the fuel of the recipe."

Coarse salt to taste
3 quarts water
¼ cup olive oil
¼ teaspoon hot red pepper flakes, or more to taste
4 cloves garlic, thinly sliced
2 tablespoons roughly chopped flat-leaf parsley leaves
1½ cups tomato sauce
1 cup chicken stock, vegetable stock, or water
Freshly ground black pepper, to taste
1 pound dried ziti

Salt the water and bring it to a boil in a large stockpot set over high heat.

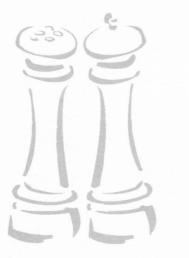

Nick Stellino's Pasta with White Mushrooms

SERVES 6 AS AN
APPETIZER OR 4 AS
A MAIN COURSE

"Get ready to see how delicious plain white mushrooms from the supermarket can be," says Nick Stellino of this recipe. To boost the mushroom flavor, Stellino suggests home cooks marinate the button mushrooms in ¼ to ½ ounce pulverized dried porcini mushrooms. The white mushrooms will soak up their essence, adding additional levels of flavor.

Meanwhile, heat the olive oil in a large sauté pan over moderate heat. Add the pepper flakes and garlic and cook 3 minutes, until the garlic begins to brown. Add 1 tablespoon of the parsley and cook for 1 minute. Add the tomato sauce and the chicken stock to the pan and season with salt and pepper. Raise the heat, bring to a boil, then lower the heat and simmer for 8 to 10 minutes.

Add the pasta to the boiling salted water and cook until al dente, 10 to 12 minutes. Reserve ¼ cup or so of the pasta's cooking water, then drain the pasta and return it to the hot pot. Pour the sauce over the pasta, raise the heat to medium-high, and toss to coat the pasta with the sauce. Pour a few tablespoons of the cooking liquid into the pot and toss again. (The starchy water will help bind the sauce.) Season with the remaining 1 tablespoon parsley and cook, stirring, for 30 to 45 seconds. Adjust the seasoning if necessary and serve immediately.

Coarse salt

6 tablespoons extra-virgin olive oil

*1 pound white mushrooms, trimmed, wiped
   clean with a damp cloth or paper towel, and
   cut into quarters*

4 cloves garlic, roughly chopped

*3 tablespoons roughly chopped flat-leaf parsley
   leaves*

³/₄ teaspoon coarse salt

³/₄ teaspoon freshly ground black pepper

¹/₂ cup white wine

2 cups chicken stock or canned broth

³/₄ cup heavy whipping cream

1 pound dried penne rigate

¹/₂ cup freshly grated Parmesan cheese

Bring a large pot of salted water to a boil over high heat.

Meanwhile, heat the olive oil in a sauté pan over high heat until almost smoking. Lower the heat to moderate, add the mushrooms to the pan, and cook until the mushrooms begin to brown, about 5 minutes. (Be careful to keep the mushrooms in a single layer, so that they cook evenly.) Stir well and cook for 3 more minutes.

Add the garlic, parsley, ¾ teaspoon salt, and the pepper to the pan and cook for another 3 minutes. Add the wine, stir well, and continue cooking until the wine is reduced by half. Add the stock and cream, raise the heat, and bring to a boil. Lower the heat and simmer for 10 minutes.

While the sauce is simmering, add the pasta to the boiling salted water and cook until al dente, 10 to 12 minutes.

Drain the cooked pasta, return it to the hot pot, pour the sauce over it, and cook over medium-low heat for 3 to 5 minutes, stirring well. Turn off the heat, adjust the seasoning if necessary, add the cheese, and stir again. Serve immediately.

Rick Moonen's Orecchiette with Cockles and Sweet Grape Tomatoes

~

SERVES 4 AS AN APPETIZER OR 2 AS A MAIN COURSE

As anyone who has ever cooked clams or mussels already knows, bivalve mollusks release intensely flavored juice when steamed open. Cockles are no different. In this recipe—based on the classic Venetian dish *spaghetti alle vongole,* or pasta with clam sauce—ear-shaped *orecchiette* is substituted for the strands of spaghetti, and cockles, standing in for clams, are steamed with copious amounts of garlic and red pepper flakes. To these Moonen adds sweet grape tomatoes, suggesting that the best time of year to make this recipe is late summer when local tomatoes are at their peak.

Precooking the pasta is another unusual step; usually the pasta and cockles (or other ingredients) are cooked simultaneously to take advantage of the binding effect of the starchy pasta water. Moonen explains how

this technique came to be: When he was *saucier* at legendary Le Cirque, one of his responsibilities was turning out the restaurant's famed pasta primavera. Because the sauce was so rich, there was no call for pasta water as a binding element. (It was also important to have the pasta cooked in advance because the dish was finished tableside.) So Moonen took to precooking the spaghetti and "shocking" it in cold water. When the restaurant management asked him to keep the pasta more al dente (firm to the bite), he began adding olive oil, letting it soak in and lending the pasta an uncommonly rich flavor and texture.

If you like, try this yourself by drizzling some olive oil (about 1/3 cup per 1 pound pasta) over the orecchiette after you've precooked it.

1/2 cup extra-virgin olive oil
2 tablespoons finely chopped red onion
2 tablespoons roughly chopped garlic
1/2 teaspoon dried oregano
1/8 teaspoon hot red pepper flakes
1/2 cup clam juice or water
1 1/2 pounds cockles (Manila, mahogany, or littleneck clams can be substituted. Increase cooking time to 5 minutes.)
1/2 pound orecchiette pasta, cooked al dente and kept warm
1 pint cherry or grape tomatoes, halved
1/2 cup roughly chopped flat-leaf parsley leaves
Coarse salt and freshly ground black pepper to taste

Warm the olive oil in a large pot over moderate heat. Add the red onion and garlic and sauté until the onion has softened but not yet colored, about 3 minutes. Add the oregano and pepper flakes and stir. Add the clam juice and cockles, cover, and steam until the cockles pop open, 2 to 3 minutes. Discard any cockles that don't open. Toss in the pasta, tomatoes, and parsley. Season with salt and pepper and serve immediately.

> *To clean cockles, cover with cold water and agitate with your hands. Drain.*

Mike Smith's Lobster and Squash Risotto

SERVES 4

When he cooked at the Blackbird restaurant in New York City, chef Mike Smith served a whole grilled lobster atop a risotto, accompanied by a ratatouille-like vegetable relish. To fit our budget, he worked the lobster into the risotto itself, making the rice the centerpiece of the meal. This is an ideal late summer dish, when lobster is at its least expensive.

This dish can also be prepared with grilled shrimp or seared scallops in place of the lobster. In the fall and winter months, think about using butternut squash or root vegetables in place of the summer squash here.

1 1¼-pound lobster, steamed, shelled, and cut into ¼-inch dice (shells reserved)

1 medium Spanish onion, cut into ¼-inch dice (skins and trimmings reserved)

2 bay leaves

2 tablespoons chopped fresh tarragon leaves (stems reserved)

1 tablespoon black peppercorns

2½ quarts water

¼ cup vegetable oil

4 summer squash, 2 green and 2 yellow, washed and cut into ½-inch dice

2 cloves garlic, mashed

2 cups Arborio rice

2 teaspoons coarse salt, plus more to taste

Freshly ground black pepper to taste

Juice of 2 lemons

3 scallions, thinly sliced

Chop the reserved lobster shells and add to a saucepan along with the onion trimmings, bay leaves, tarragon stems, and peppercorns. Cover with the water and bring to a boil over high heat. Lower the heat and simmer until the liquid is reduced to approximately 2 quarts, 15 to 20 minutes. Strain, return to the pot, and bring to a simmer.

For the risotto, place a medium saucepot over a low flame and add the oil. When the oil is warm, add the onion, summer squash, and garlic and cook until softened, 3 to 4 minutes. Add the rice and stir well to coat with oil. Season with approximately 2 teaspoons salt. Cook for 1 to 2 minutes until the oil has been absorbed by the rice.

Add one-third of the simmering lobster stock and stir well. (The trick to a creamy risotto is to stir constantly.) When almost all of the stock has been absorbed by the rice, add another one-third of the stock and continue to stir. At this point, check the seasoning and add more salt if desired. When the stock has again been almost entirely absorbed, add the remaining stock. When the rice is tender all the way through and looks creamy, add the tarragon and lobster meat and incorporate throughout. Adjust the seasoning with salt if necessary, and freshly ground black pepper if desired. Finish with fresh lemon juice and serve in warm soup bowls, garnished with the sliced scallions.

Vegetarian Main Courses

Michael Romano's Eggplant Parmigiana

SERVES 4

This is a very traditional recipe, and as with many such recipes, the key to its success lies in carefully following a few simple guidelines: Be very careful not to burn the eggplant. Make sure the oil is hot in the pan before adding the eggplant, otherwise the vegetable will absorb it. Drain the cooked eggplant on paper towels to absorb as much oil as possible. Taking these precautionary steps will ensure that the eggplant is cooked perfectly, exuding its characteristic flavor with no traces of scalding or sogginess.

2 medium eggplants (2 pounds)
1 tablespoon plus 1 teaspoon coarse salt
6 tablespoons extra-virgin olive oil
2 cloves garlic, finely minced
8 sprigs fresh basil, thinly sliced
1 28-ounce can chopped tomatoes
Freshly ground black pepper to taste
2 cups all-purpose flour
3/4 cup grated Grana Padano or Parmesan
   cheese
1 cup thinly sliced fresh mozzarella cheese

Peel the eggplants and cut across the width into ⅛-inch-thick slices. Sprinkle the slices with 1 tablespoon salt and arrange them in a colander placed over a bowl. Place a plate over the eggplant slices and allow to drain for at least 2 hours. This will rid the eggplant of its bitterness.

> GRANA PADANO
>
> This cheese is a less expensive, but serviceable, alternative to Parmigiano-Reggiano. Aged about one-third as long, it doesn't have the same sharpness as Parmesan but is a perfectly respectable grating cheese. If you want to spend a bit more money, by all means use Parmesan cheese instead.

To make the sauce, place 1 tablespoon of the olive oil and the garlic in a 3-quart saucepan over medium heat. Cook until the garlic softens, about 2 minutes, taking care to not allow the garlic to brown. Add half the sliced basil and the tomatoes with their juice to the pan and season with the remaining 1 teaspoon salt and the pepper. Allow to simmer gently for 25 minutes. Taste and adjust the seasoning if necessary. Set aside.

Heat 4 tablespoons of the remaining olive oil in a wide, heavy-bottomed skillet over

medium heat. Coat the eggplant slices with the flour and sauté them in batches until golden brown on both sides, 2 to 3 minutes per side. Drain the slices on absorbent paper towels.

Preheat the oven to 350° F.

With the remaining I tablespoon olive oil, lightly brush the bottom of a 3-quart baking dish. Ladle a small amount of the sauce on the bottom of the dish, then arrange a layer of eggplant on the sauce. Sprinkle some of the Grana Padano over the eggplant, top with another layer of sauce, and sprinkle a layer of the mozzarella over the sauce. Repeat the process until all the eggplant, sauce, and cheese are used up, making sure that the top layer is mozzarella.

Cover the casserole loosely with aluminum foil and bake in the preheated oven for 40 minutes until the eggplant is very tender and the sauce is bubbling. The eggplant may be served hot, cold, or at room temperature.

Bill Wavrin's Mushroom Potato Burgers

(adapted from the Rancho La Puerta Cookbook)

SERVES 4

This is a spa version of a burger that approximates the weight and texture of the real thing. At Rancho La Puerta spa, where Bill Wavrin is the executive chef, this burger is second in popularity only to a more classic vegetable burger made with rice and mushrooms.

This recipe came about when Wavrin went looking for a use for leftover potatoes from a dinner the previous evening. As popular as it is at the spa, however, Wavrin was skeptical about serving it up to the "Chef on a Shoestring" crew. But even our veteran staff members were surprised by the tempting aroma thrown off by these burgers as they were cooked.

As good as veggie burgers are, Wavrin says, they require some freezing to hold their shape. These, on the other hand, may be prepared à la minute, thanks to the binding elements. Wavrin likes these with a bit of Dijon mustard atop multigrain or whole-wheat bread.

¼ teaspoon extra-virgin olive oil

½ cup chopped onion

2 teaspoons minced garlic

1 cup thinly sliced white mushroom caps

⅓ cup grated carrots

1¼ cups unseasoned mashed potatoes (from 2 large russets or Idahos)

1 large egg white

2 tablespoons dry white bread crumbs

2 tablespoons ground cashews

2 scallions, thinly sliced

1½ teaspoons chopped basil leaves

¼ teaspoon minced fresh ginger

Pinch of hot red pepper flakes

Coarse salt and freshly ground black pepper to taste

4 slices whole-wheat bread

2 tablespoons Dijon mustard

½ head romaine lettuce, shredded

1 medium tomato, thinly sliced

1 red onion, thinly sliced

In a medium sauté pan, warm the olive oil over moderate heat. Add the chopped onion and the garlic to the pan and sauté until the onion is golden, about 5 minutes. Add the mushrooms and carrots and sauté, stirring occasionally, until the vegetables begin to soften, about 5 minutes. Drain off any liquid and transfer the vegetables to a large bowl.

To the bowl, add the potatoes, egg white, bread crumbs, cashews, scallions, basil, gin-ger, and pepper flakes. Season to taste with salt and pepper and mix well. The mixture should be moist.

Using an ice cream scoop, spoon out about one-fourth of the potato mixture. Between dampened palms, flatten the mixture into a patty and set aside on a tray lined with wax paper. Form another 3 patties in the same fashion.

Preheat a stovetop grill or heat a large sauté pan lightly sprayed with vegetable oil over moderate heat. Cook the patties, turning once, for about 3 minutes on each side until golden brown.

Toast the bread and spread each slice with mustard. Top with lettuce, tomato, and onion and then with a burger. Serve immediately as open-faced sandwiches.

Jeanette Maier's Hearty Root Vegetable and Lentil Stew with Three Herbs

SERVES 4

Feel free to substitute your own favorite root vegetables or alter the quantities of the ones in this recipe.

2 tablespoons extra-virgin olive oil
1 medium onion, roughly chopped
3 cloves garlic, minced
½ teaspoon dried thyme
½ teaspoon dried basil
½ teaspoon dried rosemary
12 ounces dried lentils, washed
1 28-ounce can whole peeled tomatoes
2 quarts water or vegetable or chicken stock
½ cup red wine (optional)
3 medium Idaho or russet potatoes, peeled and chopped
2 small turnips, peeled and chopped
2 small parsnips, peeled and chopped
2 small carrots, peeled and chopped
½ head cabbage, roughly chopped
Sea salt and freshly ground black pepper to taste

Warm the olive oil in a large, deep pan set over moderate heat. Add the onion, garlic, thyme, basil, and rosemary and sauté until the onion is translucent, 4 to 5 minutes. Add the lentils, tomatoes with their liquid, water, wine if desired, potatoes, turnips, parsnips, and carrots. Bring to a boil over high heat, then reduce the heat and simmer, covered, for 40 minutes. Add the cabbage and season with salt and pepper. Simmer another 10 minutes. Spoon into 4 individual soup bowls and serve immediately.

Brian Whitmer's Baked Polenta with Rosemary Roasted Portobello Mushrooms and Winter Tomato Sauce

SERVES 4

In this recipe, chef Brian Whitmer of California's The Lodge at Sonoma creates a winter tomato sauce using a combination of canned fresh and sun-dried tomatoes, complementing them with portobello mushrooms and the potent earthiness of rosemary. Presoaking the polenta will help the cornmeal loosen up and cook all the way through and will also relieve it of its grainy quality; to ensure the proper texture, add the polenta slowly as you whisk.

FOR THE POLENTA:
7 ounces coarse cornmeal
5 cups water
Coarse salt to taste
1 cup whole milk
2 tablespoons unsalted butter
Freshly ground black pepper to taste

FOR THE MUSHROOMS:
2 medium portobello mushrooms, wiped with a damp cloth and stems removed
5 to 6 sprigs rosemary
Extra-virgin olive oil, for drizzling
2 tablespoons water
Coarse salt and freshly ground black pepper to taste

FOR THE WINTER TOMATO SAUCE:
1 teaspoon extra-virgin olive oil
1/2 small yellow onion, cut into 1/4-inch dice
1 28-ounce can crushed tomatoes
1 1/2 ounces sun-dried tomatoes in oil, chopped and held in oil
1/2 teaspoon chopped fresh rosemary leaves
Pinch of sugar
Coarse salt and freshly ground black pepper to taste

3 ounces fresh goat cheese, crumbled

TO MAKE THE POLENTA:
Place the cornmeal in a mixing bowl. Bring 1 cup of the water to a boil and pour it over the cornmeal. Stir to combine and allow the mixture to sit for 15 minutes. Bring the remain-

ing 4 cups water to a boil in a saucepan and add a pinch of salt. Lower the heat to a simmer and slowly add the polenta to the saucepan, constantly whisking to combine. Cook the polenta, stirring with a wooden spoon, for about 20 minutes until it thickens like a porridge. In the final 5 minutes, add the milk and butter and season with salt and pepper to taste. Turn the thickened polenta onto a sheet pan to cool, spread it into an even layer, and refrigerate until ready to use.

TO PREPARE THE
MUSHROOMS:
Preheat the oven to 375° F.

Make a "pouch" of aluminum foil and place the mushrooms inside. Add the rosemary sprigs, drizzle with olive oil and the water, and season with salt and pepper. Seal the pouch by crimping the edges together, place it on a half-sheet pan, and bake in the preheated oven until the mushrooms are cooked through, about 30 minutes. Remove from the heat, discard the rosemary sprigs, and remove the mushrooms from the pouch. Keep the mushrooms covered and warm.

TO MAKE THE WINTER
TOMATO SAUCE:
Warm the olive oil in a saucepan over moderate heat. Add the onion, canned and sundried tomatoes, rosemary, and sugar to the pan. Season with salt and pepper and simmer for 20 minutes.

When the mushrooms are still warm but not too hot to handle, cut each mushroom in

half and then make several slices across the length of each mushroom half, but keeping one end intact. Fan out each mushroom half.

When ready to serve, preheat the broiler. Cut the polenta into decorative shapes, top each piece with crumbled cheese, and warm under the broiler until the cheese melts, about 5 minutes. Serve piping hot over the tomato sauce with the mushroom "fans" on top.

In the Studio

Every Friday morning I attend a senior news staff meeting where each producer explains what's going to be in their segment for the weekend. We discuss breaking stories and who's in the news, but when I discuss "Chef on a Shoestring," everyone leans forward just a bit to hear what the menu for the next morning's show will be. Often I'm asked by my fellow producers, and by people I meet in social situations, whether or not we really manage to make all of the recipes on the show for under $20. The answer, as you'll learn from this book, is a resounding "yes."

When we go to air on Saturday morning, the two biggest challenges we face with "Chef on a Shoestring" are how much food to buy (we need to have a second set of ingredients on hand in case a second take is called for) and how to explain and prepare a three-course meal in seven minutes. It is a challenge for the chefs, who have to chop and talk at the same time.

The shoestring segment is shot on a soundstage and managed from a nearby control room that looks like the bridge of the Starship Enterprise. Our director, Bill Brady, keeps the action moving, and is helped in this effort by the technicians who can't wait to go to commercial—so they can run out and taste the food.

—Hal Gessner

David Walzog's Black Bean Casserole

～

SERVES 4

David Walzog, of New York City's Tapika and Michael Jordan's The Steakhouse NYC, has simplified a popular dish at his restaurants for home cooks. In addition to being inexpensive, it's a great make-ahead item. Once prepared, it may be held in the refrigerator overnight, then brought to room temperature and baked in a 350° F oven for about 40 minutes. For meat eaters, Walzog recommends topping each serving of this casserole with a New York strip steak or your favorite cut of beef.

1 pound dried black beans
1 gallon water
1 tablespoon coarse salt, plus more to taste
1 large Vidalia onion, 1/2 roughly chopped and
    1/2 thinly sliced
6 sprigs cilantro
1 tablespoon olive oil
1 tablespoon unsalted butter (approximately)
3 zucchini, thinly sliced lengthwise
10 corn tortillas
3 ears corn, kernels removed
8 ounces Monterey Jack cheese, grated
1/2 bunch cilantro, stems removed, roughly
    chopped
Freshly ground black pepper to taste
3 jalapeño peppers, sliced crosswise (seeds
    removed if you prefer a less spicy dish)

Place the black beans, water, salt, chopped onion, and cilantro sprigs in a large pot and bring to a boil over high heat. Lower the heat to allow the liquid to simmer and cook for 1½ hours until the beans are soft. Drain the beans, reserving 1 quart of the cooking liquid. Allow the beans to cool slightly. Purée the beans with the reserved liquid in a blender until smooth. (You may need to do this in batches.)

While the beans are cooking, warm the olive oil in a sauté pan set over moderate heat. Add the sliced onion and sauté until softened and translucent, 4 to 5 minutes. Remove from the heat and set aside.

Preheat the oven to 350° F.

Butter a 12-inch baking dish. Line the bottom of the dish with a layer of zucchini strips. On top of the zucchini, place a layer of corn tortillas, followed by a layer of corn kernels, then a layer of sautéed onion, a layer of black bean purée, a layer of Jack cheese, and finally a layer of chopped cilantro. Season with salt and pepper. Continue layering the casserole in this order until the baking dish is full. Garnish the top of the casserole with cheese and sliced jalapeños. Bake in the preheated oven for 1 hour. Remove from the oven and serve immediately.

David Walzog's Asparagus and Cremini Mushroom Barley "Risotto"

SERVES 4

Risotto has become very familiar to contemporary American diners, but it often remains a bit intimidating to home cooks.

In what he refers to as a "dummy-proof" risotto, chef David Walzog substitutes pearl barley for the Arborio rice. "Because barley doesn't have the same starch content," Walzog explains, "the stirring points aren't so vital in the end. You can make this on the wet side and simply cook out any excess liquid in the pan."

At his restaurants, Walzog employs his risotto as a component to a variety of meat dishes. He encourages readers to do as he does and freely substitute other vegetables for the asparagus and mushrooms—either to accommodate seasonal availability or the other dishes on your menu.

3 cups pearl barley
2 quarts water

2 tablespoons coarse salt, plus more to taste

1 bunch large asparagus, peeled, 4 stalks
   reserved for garnish and the remaining cut
   crosswise into $\frac{1}{8}$-inch slices

$\frac{1}{4}$ cup corn oil

8 ounces cremini mushrooms, sliced $\frac{1}{4}$ inch
   thick

1 cup finely diced Vidalia onion

$\frac{1}{4}$ cup heavy cream

1 tablespoon roughly chopped cilantro leaves

1 tablespoon unsalted butter

Freshly ground black pepper to taste

Combine the barley and water in a large pot. Add 2 tablespoons coarse salt to the pot. Bring the water to a boil over high heat. Lower the heat to let the water simmer and continue to simmer until the barley is tender and soft, about 45 minutes. Drain the barley and keep warm in a covered bowl.

While the barley is cooking, bring a small pot of salted water to a boil. Prepare an ice water bath (see page 227). Blanch the whole asparagus stalks in boiling water for 30 seconds, then remove to the ice water bath to "shock" the asparagus and preserve its color. Remove from the cold water, pat dry, and reserve.

In a 3-quart sauté pan, warm the corn oil over high heat for 1 minute. Add the mushrooms, chopped asparagus, and onion and sauté for 3 minutes over high heat. Add the barley to the vegetables and mix thoroughly with a mixing spoon. Add the cream, cilantro, and butter and stir well for 45 seconds over medium heat. Season with salt and pepper.

Spoon equal portions of the prepared risotto into individual serving dishes and garnish with the blanched asparagus.

Fish
and
Seafood

Amanda Hesser's Mussels with Garlic and Fresh Herbs

(*adapted from* The Cook and the Gardener, *W. W. Norton & Company, 1999*)

～

SERVES 4 TO 6

Amanda Hesser bases this recipe on the classic *moules marinière,* in which mussels are cooked in a broth of white wine, shallots, parsley, and butter. She adds tarragon to the mix, taking advantage of the affinity it enjoys with seafood, and replaces the butter with olive oil to lend the dish a fresher, clean taste. However, if you prefer, you can use butter instead of olive oil to emulsify the juices and enrich the sauce.

3 pounds mussels
1$^1/_2$ cups white wine
4 shallot lobes, thinly sliced
1 bay leaf
2 tablespoons extra-virgin olive oil
2 cloves garlic, thinly sliced
1 tablespoon chopped flat-leaf parsley leaves
2 teaspoons chopped tarragon leaves
1 baguette, for serving

Special equipment: coffee filter or cheesecloth

Clean the mussels by scrubbing them well under cold running water. Debeard them if necessary by pulling out any wiry fronds coming through the seams of the shells.

In a large pot or deep sauté pan, combine the wine, half the shallots, and the bay leaf. Place the mussels on top and cover with a lid. Bring to a boil over high heat to steam open the mussels, 3 to 4 minutes. You may want to give them a stir after 2 minutes to disperse the heat evenly among the mussels. When the mussels have opened, transfer them to 4 shallow bowls. Discard any mussels that don't open; this is an indication that they are dead or bad.

Strain the cooking liquid through a coffee filter or several layers of cheesecloth into a clean pan. Add the olive oil, remaining shallot, and the garlic and bring to a boil over medium-high heat. Reduce the mixture slightly; it will condense to an opaque liquid after 3 to 5 minutes. Taste. If it's too salty, add a little water. Sprinkle the herbs and spoon the sauce over the mussels. Serve promptly with a tangy baguette torn into large pieces, which you can use to soak up the broth when you're finished with the mussels.

Erik Blauberg's Spanish Mackerel with Sautéed Potatoes, Cremini Mushrooms, and Spicy Tomatoes

SERVES 4

In this Mediterranean-style dish, chef Erik Blauberg uses the confit technique to braise Spanish mackerel in a pot of oil that's flavored with tomato, garlic, rosemary, and thyme. The flavors are imparted to the fish, and complemented by jalapeño peppers. For a more luxurious result, use extra-virgin olive oil instead of canola oil.

2 medium Idaho or russet potatoes

2 cups plus 4 tablespoons canola oil

2 sprigs fresh rosemary, or 1½ tablespoons dried

2 sprigs fresh thyme, or 1½ tablespoons dried

1 plum tomato

2 cloves garlic, unpeeled

Coarse salt and freshly ground black pepper to taste

2 1¼-pound Spanish mackerel or other favorite white fish, filleted and skinned, cut into 8 equal pieces

Coarse salt

1 cup thinly sliced cremini mushrooms

4 vine-ripened tomatoes, cut into ¼-inch dice

1 jalapeño pepper, seeded and cut into small dice

3 tablespoons balsamic vinegar

1 teaspoon chopped orange zest

Preheat the oven to 350° F.

Cook the potatoes in a pot of boiling salted water for 10 minutes. Drain, and when cool enough to handle, slice into ⅛-inch-thick rounds.

Place 2 cups of the oil in a deep saucepot. Add the herbs, whole tomato, and the garlic to the pot and season with salt and pepper. Place the fish fillets in the pot and place the pot in the preheated oven. Cook for 8 to 10 minutes until the fish is opaque in the center. Remove from the oven. Set aside and keep warm.

Meanwhile, warm 2 tablespoons of the remaining oil in a sauté pan over moderate heat. Add the potatoes to the pan and cook until lightly browned on both sides, 2 to 3 minutes per side. Remove from the heat, drain on paper towels, and keep warm.

Pour the remaining 2 tablespoons oil into the same sauté pan and heat over moderate heat. Add the mushrooms and cook for 1 minute. Add the tomatoes and jalapeño and cook for 1 additional minute. Remove from the heat, add the balsamic vinegar to the pan, and stir to combine. Season with salt and pepper.

To assemble, arrange the potatoes in the center of each of 4 dinner plates. Top with the tomato mixture, then with 2 fish pieces. Sprinkle with orange zest and serve immediately.

Eric Ripert's Shrimp Tabbouleh

SERVES 4 TO 6

A Middle Eastern recipe may seem out of character for a four-star New York City restaurant with a French chef at the helm, but this Lebanese staple is a summertime offering at Le Bernardin, where the bulgur wheat of the original is replaced with delicate pearls of couscous that lend the tabbouleh a very full and satisfying mouth-feel. Sautéed shrimp are added to make what is normally a vegetarian dish fit in with the restaurant's reputation for world-class seafood. Presented here warm, the tabbouleh (and shrimp) may also be served chilled, as it traditionally is.

At the restaurant, Ripert adds diced red and green peppers and coriander to the tabbouleh and often uses more luxurious lobster instead of shrimp.

1 cup water
8 tablespoons extra-virgin olive oil
Coarse salt and freshly ground black pepper to taste
1/2 cup couscous
2 beefsteak tomatoes, peeled, seeded, and diced (page 227)
1 cucumber, peeled, seeded, and cut into 1/4-inch dice
1 teaspoon roughly chopped flat-leaf parsley leaves
2 teaspoons roughly chopped fresh mint leaves, plus 8 sprigs for garnish
Juice of 1 lemon
8 ounces tiny shrimp

Combine the water and 3 tablespoons of the olive oil in a medium saucepot. Season with salt and pepper and bring to a boil over high heat. Add the couscous and stir to combine. Lower the heat to moderate, cover, and let steam for 5 minutes until all the water has been absorbed. Stir again and let cool.

In a separate bowl, combine the tomatoes, cucumber, parsley, and mint.

When the couscous is cool, add it to the tomato mixture, along with the lemon juice and 2 tablespoons of the remaining olive oil. Mix to combine well and season to taste with salt and pepper.

Season the shrimp liberally with salt and pepper and sauté in a large pan or skillet in the remaining 3 tablespoons olive oil over moderate heat until they turn pink and are firm to the touch. (You may need to do this in batches.)

Divide the couscous mixture evenly among 4 plates and top with the sautéed shrimp. Garnish with mint sprigs. Serve immediately.

Alfred Portale's Cod with Brussels Sprouts, Yukon Gold Potatoes, and Onions

SERVES 4

This dish demonstrates the fiscal benefits of buying in-season ingredients—in this case, Brussels sprouts. Americans don't have much affection for Brussels sprouts, but Portale believes that this may be because we most often eat them whole. But if cored (see Note) and the leaves are cooked in boiling salted water, the sprouts retain their appealing pale green color, and their sweet flavor may surprise you.

Coarse salt to taste

1 pound Yukon Gold potatoes

1 carrot, cut into ¼-inch dice

6 ounces boiling onions, cut into ¼-inch slices

8 ounces Brussels sprouts, cored and separated into leaves (see Note)

1 cup chicken stock

½ cup heavy cream

Freshly ground black pepper to taste

Bring cold salted water to a boil in a large, heavy-bottomed pot. Add the potatoes to the pot and cook until tender when pierced with the tip of a knife, 10 to 15 minutes.

While the potatoes are cooking, bring a separate pot of cold salted water to a boil. (You will be cooking the carrots in this pot.) Also prepare an ice water bath (see page 227).

When the potatoes are done, drain and set aside to cool. When the potatoes are cool enough to work with, cut them crosswise into ½-inch-thick rounds and set aside.

Cook the carrot in the boiling water until barely tender, approximately 2 minutes. Remove the carrot from the water and reserve. Add the onions to the pot of boiling water and cook until barely tender, approximately 2 minutes. Remove and reserve. Cook the Brussels sprout leaves in the same pot of boiling water until barely tender, 2 to 3 minutes. Drain and shock in the ice water bath. Using your hands, squeeze out all excess moisture from the leaves and blot on a kitchen towel.

In a medium-size sauce pot, bring the chicken stock and cream to a boil over high heat. Reduce the liquid by one-third. Add the potatoes, carrots, onions, and Brussels sprouts to the pot. Reduce the heat to low and simmer for 5 minutes. Season with salt and pepper to taste and keep warm.

For the cod:

4 cod fillets (4 to 6 ounces each)

Coarse salt and freshly ground black pepper to taste

3 tablespoons canola oil

Season the cod on both sides with salt and pepper. Heat the oil in a 12-inch sauté pan over medium-high heat. Place the cod in the pan and cook until golden brown, approximately 3 minutes. Turn and cook the other side approximately 3 minutes. Reduce the heat to medium and continue cooking until the cod is opaque in the center, approximately 3 minutes.

Transfer the vegetables to a warmed serving platter or individual plates using a slotted spoon. Arrange the cod fillets on top of the vegetables and spoon extra sauce around the vegetables and fish. Serve immediately.

NOTE: Core Brussels sprouts with a sharp, thin-bladed knife (like a paring knife), then separate the individual leaves.

Rick Moonen's Salmon Burgers with Green Tartar Sauce

SERVES 4

"I'm not a griddle burger kind of guy," proclaims Rick Moonen with characteristic down-to-earth enthusiasm. "I like the smoky flavor you can only get with a real outdoor grill." But to create a burger out of salmon, this inventive chef makes some concessions to adjust for the likelihood that a fish patty would break apart on the grate of an outdoor grill.

Moonen cubes salmon and combines it with bell peppers, scallions, and Tabasco sauce, adding a foamy whipped egg white to bind it all together. You may substitute tuna, crab, or shrimp for the salmon. The resulting mixture should resemble a tartare. The burger is browned on the stovetop, heated through in the oven, then flipped and finished on the burner.

The mayonnaise-based green tartar sauce is sparked by an herbaceous mix of dill, chives, and parsley—all classic salmon accompaniments. Finally, Moonen manages to sneak in a bit of his beloved char-flavor

by grilling Indian *naan* or Middle Eastern pita bread and using it as the "bun" for this unique seafood burger.

Green Tartar Sauce (recipe follows)
4 pieces tandori naan *or thick pita bread*
2 tablespoons extra-virgin olive oil
   (approximately)
1 pound salmon, skin and bones removed, cut
   into ¼-inch dice
½ cup green bell pepper, seeded and cut into ¼-
   inch dice
¼ cup chopped scallions (use all but the very
   tops)
¼ cup heavy cream
1 teaspoon Tabasco sauce
Coarse salt and freshly ground black pepper to
   taste
1 large egg white
1 tablespoon vegetable oil
2 teaspoons unsalted butter
1 ripe beefsteak tomato, cut into 4 slices
4 to 8 leaves red leaf lettuce, shredded

Preheat the broiler. Lightly brush each side of the bread with olive oil. Place under broiler and cook until brown, about 2 minutes. Carefully turn the bread over and broil another 2 minutes. Remove the bread to a cutting board. (Do not turn off the broiler.) When cool enough to handle, trim the ends to form squares and cut each square in half to yield 8 slices. (If using pita bread, cut each piece in half then trim about 1 inch off the pointed corners on each piece.)

Put the salmon in a mixing bowl. Add the

green pepper, scallions, and cream and combine well. Stir in the Tabasco sauce and season with salt and pepper. In a separate bowl, beat the egg white with a whisk until soft peaks form and gently fold half of the egg white into the salmon mixture. Continue to add the egg white until the mixture is bound together, being careful not to let it become soggy. Season with salt and pepper and fold to combine one last time. Form 4 patties that are 4 inches across and about ¾ inch thick.

Preheat a large nonstick ovenproof skillet over medium-high heat until hot. Add the vegetable oil and swirl to evenly coat the bottom of the pan. Add the salmon burgers to the pan, lower the heat to medium, and place ½ teaspoon butter next to each burger. Sauté until browned, 2 to 3 minutes. Carefully turn the burgers over and cook under the broiler for 1 minute. Return to the stovetop and cook over medium heat for an additional 2 minutes.

Arrange each burger on a slice of bread. Top with a thick slice of tomato, 1 heaping tablespoon tartar sauce, ¼ cup red leaf lettuce, and finish with another slice of bread. Serve warm.

Green Tartar Sauce

¼ cup chopped cornichons or dill pickles (optional)
1½ tablespoons capers (optional)
1 large shallot, cut into ¼-inch dice (about ¼ cup)
⅔ cup mayonnaise
2½ tablespoons roughly chopped flat-leaf parsley leaves
1½ tablespoons roughly chopped fresh dill leaves
2 teaspoons lemon juice
½ teaspoon Dijon mustard
½ teaspoon freshly ground black pepper
¼ cup olive oil

For the tartar sauce, if using cornichons and/or capers, place them with the shallots in a food processor and pulse once or twice just to combine the ingredients. Add the mayonnaise, parsley, dill, lemon juice, mustard, and pepper and process well to blend thoroughly. Open the pour spout on the processor and, with the motor running, slowly add the oil in a thin stream to form a thick, emulsified sauce. Transfer the tartar sauce to an airtight container and refrigerate, preferably overnight, to allow the flavors to blend. The tartar sauce should be made 1 day ahead to allow the flavors to develop before serving. The extra sauce can be used on sandwiches or with sautéed fish.

Paul Opitz's Bay Scallops and Crab Meat à la Chesapeake

SERVES 4

The word "Chesapeake" in the title of this New England recipe refers to the combination of crab and cream. Paul Opitz, of Phillips Seafood, warns home cooks to be careful not to overcook the scallops because they will harden in the casserole. Also take care not to overthicken the sauce, or the dish will have an unpleasant gluey texture.

½ cup (1 stick) unsalted butter

2 large cloves garlic, minced

1 bunch scallions, tops and root ends trimmed, thinly sliced

1 pound bay scallops

8 ounces hand-picked crab claw meat

¾ cup heavy cream

1 ounce (2½ tablespoons) cornstarch or arrowroot dissolved in ½ cup water

Coarse salt and freshly ground black pepper, to taste

6 tablespoons sherry

Juice of ½ lemon

1 pound fresh, colorful garden vegetables, such as snow peas, sliced carrots, broccoli, steamed or sautéed according to your personal taste

1 box (8 ounces) couscous, cooked according to package directions

Preheat the oven to 400° F.

Melt the butter in a saucepan over moderate heat. Add the garlic and scallions and sauté until the scallions are wilted, 2 to 3 minutes. Add the scallops and cook, stirring occasionally, over high heat until the scallops weep, about 5 minutes. Add the crab meat and stir for 30 seconds to warm and incorporate. Remove from the heat, pour off and reserve any liquid in the pan, and set aside the seafood mixture.

Heat the reserved liquid in a small saucepan over moderate heat. Add the cream and dissolved cornstarch and season with salt and pepper. Bring to a boil. Lower the heat, add the sherry, and cook until thick enough to coat a wooden spoon. Add a pinch more cornstarch if the liquid appears too runny, adding some lemon juice, if necessary, to wake up the flavors. Adjust the seasoning to taste. Divide the seafood mixture among 4 small ovenproof casseroles. Cover evenly with the sauce and bake for 20 minutes in the preheated oven.

Serve with the fresh vegetables and couscous.

Michael Lomonaco's Pan-Roasted Halibut with Spring Vegetables

SERVES 4

This "market dish" allows each cook to express his or her individual creativity and personal taste by substituting different vegetables for the ones in the recipe. The rendition featured below suits spring or early summer because that's when favas and asparagus are at the height of their season. Even in these months, however, any fresh shell bean, or even English peas, may be substituted.

In the fall and winter months, make this dish with fresh broad beans and Swiss chard. You may also substitute cod or Chilean sea bass for the halibut.

1½ pounds halibut fillet, ¾ inch thick, cut into 4 pieces
Coarse salt and freshly ground black pepper to taste
2 tablespoons extra-virgin olive oil
1 cup blanched pencil-thin asparagus tips
½ cup shelled blanched fresh fava beans
⅓ cup dry white wine
2 to 3 tablespoons unsalted butter
1 to 2 tablespoons chopped tarragon leaves

Season the halibut on both sides with salt and pepper. In a casserole or skillet, heat the oil over moderate heat. Add the fish, flesh side down, and sauté for 4 minutes. Turn the fish and sauté, skin side down, for 4 minutes. Add the asparagus and fava beans to the skillet with the fish and cook for 2 minutes. Add the wine, partially cover, and cook for 1 minute more. Remove the fish to a serving platter. Stir the butter and tarragon into the pan with the vegetables and spoon the sauce over the fish. Serve immediately.

David Reardon's Pan-Seared Scallops and Oyster Mushroom Sweet Potato Salad with Cilantro Ginger Vinaigrette

⁓

SERVES 4

David Reardon, the executive chef of the W Hotel in Honolulu, became a fan of scallops in his hometown of Boston. In this dish, he takes advantage of their sweetness, complementing it with ginger, cilantro, and sweet potatoes. This recipe was inspired by the herb-crusted Hawaiian prawn with Yukon Gold and mushroom salad that he offers at the W Hotel.

4 U-10 sea scallops (less than 10 to a pound)
Coarse salt and freshly ground white pepper to taste
2 tablespoons extra-virgin olive oil
2 tablespoons finely diced yellow onion
1 teaspoon minced garlic
1 medium sweet potato, peeled, cut into 1-inch cubes, and blanched (1 cup)
4 ounces oyster mushrooms, wiped with a damp cloth
David Reardon's Cilantro Ginger Vinaigrette (recipe follows)

Season the scallops on both sides with salt and pepper.

Heat a sauté pan over moderate heat. Add 1 tablespoon of the olive oil to the pan and heat it until almost smoking. Place the scallops in the pan and sear them until golden brown on each side, about 1 minute per side. Remove the scallops from the pan and keep warm.

Add the remaining 1 tablespoon oil to the pan. Add the onion and cook, stirring, for 30 seconds. Add the garlic, sweet potato, and mushrooms and sauté until the vegetables are cooked, 3 to 4 minutes, being careful not to burn or brown the garlic. Remove from the heat, add 2 tablespoons of the vinaigrette to the pan, and stir well to combine. Place a generous spoonful of the sweet potato mixture in the center of each of 4 warmed salad plates and top with the scallops. Drizzle the remaining vinaigrette over the scallops and on the plates.

David Reardon's Cilantro Ginger Vinaigrette

MAKES ABOUT ¹/₂ CUP

In addition to the preceding scallop recipe, this vinaigrette is also delicious with salads, grilled fish, and grilled pork medallions.

1¹/₂ tablespoons red wine vinegar
¹/₂ teaspoon Dijon mustard
6 tablespoons extra-virgin olive oil
1 teaspoon grated fresh ginger
1 tablespoon finely chopped cilantro
Coarse salt and freshly ground black pepper to
    taste

In a small bowl, whisk together the vinegar and the mustard. Gradually add the olive oil, whisking, until the mixture is emulsified. Add the ginger and cilantro and season to taste with salt and pepper.

Henry Meer's Brook Trout Steamed with Vegetables

SERVES 4

In the classic preparation of fish cooked *en papillote*, a fillet—usually accompanied by a variety of vegetables—is baked in a heart-shaped parchment-paper envelope. Most home cooks probably don't have parchment paper on hand, but Henry Meer, executive chef and owner of New York City's Cub Room and City Hall, offers a less intimidating, but no less effective, method using aluminum foil instead. Meer finds that this "easy, no mess" technique offers a great way to prepare dinner in advance and cook it quickly when ready to eat. "It's good for bachelors, or people tired of TV dinners," he says.

When they're in season, you might add or substitute tomatoes, zucchini, asparagus, and/or snow peas to the vegetable mix. Just about any flaky white fish will work in this recipe. If you're loosening up the budget, try it with halibut, turbot, or sole.

2 tablespoons canola or vegetable oil

4 carrots, julienned

4 celery stalks, julienned

8 thin slices fresh ginger, each 1 to 2 inches long

4 cloves of garlic, germ removed, finely sliced

1 large onion, peeled and cut into 8 slices

1 red bell pepper, julienned

2 large white mushrooms, thinly sliced

2 baby bok choy, thinly sliced

1 large lemon, cut into 8 thin slices, seeds discarded

2 limes, cut into 8 thin slices, seeds discarded

4 7-ounce brook trout fillets

2 tablespoons extra-virgin olive oil (approximately)

4 sprigs basil

4 sprigs cilantro

Coarse salt and freshly ground black pepper to taste

Preheat the oven to 350° F.

In a medium-size sauté pan, warm the vegetable oil over medium heat and cook the carrots, celery, ginger, garlic, onion, and red pepper, stirring constantly, for 3 minutes. Add the mushrooms and bok choy and sauté, continuing to stir, until all the vegetables are wilted, 4 to 6 minutes. Remove the vegetables from the heat.

Place 2 lemon slices and 2 lime slices on top of each fish fillet. Brush 4 pieces of aluminum foil, each about 12 inches long, lightly with olive oil. Make an envelope out of the foil and place each fish fillet with lemon and lime in its own envelope. Distrib-ute the cooked vegetables evenly among the envelopes on top of the fillets. Place the sprigs of basil and cilantro on top. Season with salt and pepper.

Seal each envelope tightly by crimping the foil together above the fish. Place the envelopes on a baking sheet and bake in the preheated oven for 8 minutes. Open carefully; the steam is very hot. Place each fish fillet with its vegetables on a warm plate and serve immediately.

Tom Douglas's Crispy Fried Snapper with Chile Ponzu

SERVES 4

This crispy fried snapper is a fun meal for casual dinners because each guest can dip pieces of fish into their own bowl of ponzu sauce. If you have trouble finding serrano and Fresno chilies or don't enjoy their flavor, feel free to substitute jalapeño, Anaheim, or pasilla peppers to attain a flavor and heat that's to your own personal taste.

2 1-pound red snappers, scales removed (ask your fishmonger to do this)
Citrus Marinade (recipe follows)
1 cup cornstarch
1 cup vegetable oil
2 cups roughly chopped cilantro leaves
Ponzu Sauce (recipe follows)

Make several slices into the sides of the fish and place in a shallow dish. Pour the marinade over the fish, being sure it finds its way into all of the sliced areas. Allow the fish to marinate, covered, overnight in the refrigerator.

When ready to cook, sprinkle the cornstarch on a plate large enough to hold one of the fish. In a skillet large enough to hold the fish, warm the oil over moderate heat until smoking. Remove 1 fish from the marinade and coat with the cornstarch, being sure to cover both sides completely. Press the cornstarch gently onto the fish to ensure that it sticks. Place the fish in the oil and fry until crispy and brown on both sides, 3 to 5 minutes per side. Remove to drain on paper towels and repeat with the other fish.

To serve, place both fish on a platter and sprinkle with the cilantro. Serve from the center of the table, giving each person their own bowl of dipping sauce. Dunk bite-size pieces of fish into the ponzu and enjoy.

Citrus Marinade

Juice of 1 orange or tangerine
Grated zest of 1 orange or tangerine
1 tablespoon soy sauce
2 tablespoons grated fresh ginger
1 cup water

Whisk together all the ingredients in a bowl.

Ponzu Sauce

Juice of 1 lime
Grated zest of 1 lime
1 tablespoon honey
2 serrano chilies, seeded and sliced
2 Fresno chilies, seemed and sliced

Combine all the ingredients in a bowl and allow to sit at room temperature for at least 1 hour. Divide among 4 small bowls.

Marcus Samuelsson's Horseradish-Baked Salmon with Carrot-Ginger Broth and Mussels

SERVES 4

This dish, a mélange of international influences, shows how the life of a chef may be reflected in his or her cuisine. In this case, Aquavit's Marcus Samuelsson, a native of Ethiopia who was raised in Sweden before traveling the world on his way to New York City, combines Swedish, French, and Thai techniques and ingredients—horseradish-baked fish from his Swedish upbringing, steamed mussels from Paris, and a carrot-ginger broth inspired by his visits to Thailand.

The extreme quantity of horseradish in this dish is no mistake; when baked, the flavor mellows and sweetens. Also, as in salt-baked fish recipes, the horseradish will harden over the salmon, creating a crust of sorts that helps the fish retain its moisture when cooked.

FOR THE BROTH AND MUSSELS:

1½ teaspoons canola oil

2 carrots, peeled, thinly sliced, slices cut into ½-inch pieces

1 small piece ginger, peeled, thinly sliced, slices cut into ½-inch pieces

1 shallot, finely chopped

3 cloves garlic, minced

1 pound mussels, scrubbed and debearded (see page 127)

4 cups bottled clam juice or water

Coarse salt and freshly ground black pepper to taste

FOR THE SALMON AND RICE:

1 cup long-grain rice

1 shallot, finely diced

3 cloves garlic, minced

2 cups cold water

1 pound salmon or salmon trout, skin removed (ask your fishmonger to divide into four 4-ounce steaks)

Juice of 1 lemon

Coarse salt and freshly ground black pepper to taste

1 cup freshly grated horseradish root

TO MAKE THE BROTH AND MUSSELS:

In a large sauté pan, heat the canola oil over medium-high heat. Add the carrots, ginger, shallot, and garlic and cook for approximately 10 minutes. Add the mussels and 2 cups of the clam juice and continue cooking, covered, until the mussels open fully, 2 to 3 minutes. Gently remove the mussels from the pan using a slotted spoon and keep warm. Discard any mussels that do not open.

Remove the pan from the heat, let cool slightly, then purée the vegetable mixture in a food processor. (You may need to work in batches.) Add as much of the remaining 2 cups clam juice as necessary to achieve a soupy consistency. Season to taste with salt and pepper. Reserve.

TO MAKE THE SALMON AND RICE (THIS SHOULD BE DONE AS THE MUSSELS AND BROTH ARE COOKING):

Preheat the oven to 350° F.

Combine the rice with the shallot, garlic, and the water in a small saucepan. Cover and cook for approximately 20 minutes over moderate heat. Remove from the heat and set aside.

While the rice is cooking, place the salmon steaks in a baking dish. Brush them with the lemon juice and season liberally with coarse salt and freshly ground black pepper. Spread the grated horseradish over each piece of salmon. Bake in the preheated oven until the horseradish is golden brown, about 6 minutes.

TO SERVE:

Gently reheat the carrot-ginger broth. Mound equal portions of rice in the center of 4 large serving bowls. Arrange the salmon on top of the rice and distribute the mussels around the perimeter. Finish by spooning the carrot-ginger broth over and around the salmon.

Richard Vellante's Polenta-Crusted Salmon with Fall Vegetables and Chestnuts

SERVES 4

When we asked Legal Sea Foods' corporate chef Rich Vellante to prepare a seafood Thanksgiving dinner, he met the challenge with a wonderful creative spirit. He began with salmon, which was an abundant fish in colonial times, and added polenta, which, of course, is made of cornmeal, evoking maize and other bounty of the first Thanksgiving table. Roasted chestnuts completed the holiday motif.

¼ cup finely chopped onions
6 tablespoons (¾ stick) unsalted butter
1 cup milk
Coarse salt and freshly ground black pepper, to taste
1 tablespoon chopped fresh tarragon
¼ cup instant polenta
1½ pounds salmon fillets, cut into 4 6-ounce portions
4 ounces Brussels sprouts, trimmed
½ butternut squash, peeled, seeded, and cut into ⅛-inch-thick slices
1 sweet potato, peeled and cut into ¼-inch dice
4 ounces pearl onions, skinned
2 sprigs rosemary
3 beets, boiled, peeled, and quartered
1 cup plus 1 tablespoon extra-virgin olive oil
¼ cup red wine vinegar
4 ounces chestnuts, roasted and finely chopped (see box, page 145)

In a saucepot, combine the chopped onion with 1 tablespoon of the butter. Add the milk, a pinch of salt, pepper to taste and the tarragon to the saucepot. Place the saucepot over high heat and bring to a boil. Add the polenta to the pot, stir well, lower the heat, and cook over low heat for 5 minutes. Finish the polenta by stirring in 1 tablespoon butter. Remove the pot from the heat and let cool until the polenta is firm but not set.

Season the salmon on both sides with salt and pepper and spread a ¼-inch-thick layer of cooled polenta on top of each fillet, using a rubber spatula and taking care not to damage the delicate fish. Cover and refrigerate for at least 30 minutes or as long as 6 hours.

Preheat the oven to 400° F.

CHESTNUTS

To roast chestnuts, cut an "X" in the bottom of each chestnut and place on a baking sheet. Roast in a preheated 375° F oven for about 25 minutes. When cool enough to handle, peel using a paring knife or chestnut knife. You might also purchase frozen peeled chestnuts from a specialty market, which will save you the hassle of removing the skins from fresh ones.

Heat 3 tablespoons butter in an ovenproof sauté pan or skillet over high heat. Add the Brussels sprouts, squash, sweet potato, pearl onions, and rosemary to the pan. Sear the vegetables, turning them as their sides brown, about 3 minutes total. Place in preheated oven and cook for 12 to 15 minutes.

Season the vegetables with salt and pepper and transfer to a roasting pan. Add the beets to the roasting pan and roast the vegetables in the preheated oven for 30 minutes.

Meanwhile, make the vinaigrette by slowly whisking 1 cup extra-virgin olive oil into the red wine vinegar until an emulsified dressing is formed. Stir in the chestnuts and season with salt and pepper.

After the vegetables have been cooking for about 20 minutes, cook the salmon: Place the remaining 1 tablespoon butter and 1 tablespoon olive oil in a nonstick sauté pan. Warm the butter and oil over moderate heat and add the salmon, polenta side down, to the pan. Cook for 5 minutes until lightly browned. Turn the salmon over and cook for an additional 3 minutes.

Remove the vegetables from the oven and discard the rosemary sprigs. Arrange the roasted vegetables decoratively on each of 4 dinner plates. Place 1 piece salmon in the center of each plate and drizzle the vinaigrette over the fish and the vegetables. Serve immediately.

Kerry Heffernan's Skate with Sautéed Beet Greens and Boiled Potatoes

SERVES 4

Skate has been on the menu at Eleven Madison Park in New York City from the day it first opened its doors. At the restaurant, chef Heffernan adds plump caper berries to the sauce. When purchasing the skate for this recipe, look for one with a skin color closer to brown than gray.

4 Yukon Gold potatoes, washed
Herb stems, such as thyme and marjoram (perhaps from Kerry Heffernan's Roasted Root Vegetable Salad, page 66)
2 cloves garlic, halved and peeled
1¹⁄₂ pounds skate on the bone, rinsed and dried
Coarse salt and freshly ground black pepper to taste
All-purpose flour, for coating
3 tablespoons grape seed oil or canola oil
1 bunch beet greens, washed, dried, and tough stems removed (Swiss chard or spinach may be substituted)
8 tablespoons (1 stick) unsalted butter
¹⁄₄ cup water
1 lemon, peeled, seeded, and thinly sliced (reserve any juice given off while slicing)
5 sprigs parsley, roughly chopped

Place the potatoes in a large pot and cover with water. Add the herb stems and garlic to the pot and bring the water to a boil over medium-high heat. Lower the heat and simmer until the potatoes are tender, 15 to 30 minutes.

Meanwhile, rinse the skate fillets and thoroughly pat them dry. Season with salt and pepper and coat lightly with the flour.

Preheat the oven to 425° F.

Place an ovenproof sauté pan large enough to hold all the fish without crowding over high heat. When the pan is very hot, add the oil and heat it until almost smoking. Place the skate, light side up, in the pan and cook until brown, about 3 to 4 minutes. Turn the fish over and bake for 10 additional minutes, or until the fish is cooked. (The fish is done when it begins to fall away from the bone and turns opaque in color.)

While the skate is browning on the stovetop, heat another skillet until very hot. Add the beet greens, 2 tablespoons of the butter, and the water to the pan. Season with salt and pepper. Sauté, stirring the greens frequently, until tender, 4 to 7 minutes. Remove from the heat and distribute the cooked greens evenly among 4 dinner plates.

When the potatoes are done, drain them, discard the garlic and herb stems, and cut them in half. Place 2 halves on each plate with the beet greens.

Remove the skate from its pan and distribute among the plates, overlaying the greens and potatoes, so that a bit of each component is showing.

Wipe out the skate sauté pan with paper towels and return it to the heat. When the pan is hot, add the remaining 6 tablespoons butter. When the butter has browned and is foaming, add the lemon slices and juice and parsley. Toss quickly, season with salt and pepper, and pour over the skate and vegetables. Serve immediately.

Joseph Tucker's Tuna Sambuca

⁓

SERVES 4

The powerful and spicy aroma given off by this unique tuna dish made quite an impression on our hosts when Philadelphia's Joseph Tucker of Pompeii restaurant visited our show. If you don't want to use alcohol or don't have any sambuca on hand, substitute an equivalent amount of honey. You can also substitute grouper or red snapper for the tuna.

2 red bell peppers
7 tablespoons olive oil
Coarse salt and freshly ground black pepper to taste
1 pound fresh tuna steak
Joseph Tucker's Blackening Seasoning Mix (recipe follows)
2 cloves garlic, finely chopped
1/2 cup pitted Kalamata olives
1/2 cup thinly sliced white button mushrooms
1 tablespoon unsalted butter
1 cup fish stock or chicken broth
4 basil leaves, roughly chopped
6 tablespoons sambuca

Preheat the oven to 350° F.

Cut the red peppers in half and discard the ribs, stems, and seeds. Julienne the peppers and place in a shallow baking dish. Sprinkle with 2 tablespoons of the olive oil and season with salt and pepper. Place the baking dish in the preheated oven and cook until the peppers are soft, approximately 20 minutes. Remove the peppers from the oven.

Meanwhile, rinse the tuna, pat dry with paper towels, and coat with the seasoning mix. Pour 4 tablespoons of the remaining olive oil into a sauté pan and heat over moderate heat until the oil is hot but not smoking. Place the tuna in the pan and cook for 1 minute on each side. Remove the tuna from the pan and set aside.

When the red peppers have been removed from the oven, discard the oil from the sauté pan in which the tuna was cooked and add the remaining 1 tablespoon fresh olive oil. Heat over medium-high heat, then add the roasted peppers, garlic, olives, and mushrooms. Sauté until the mushrooms soften, about 3 minutes. Add the butter and fish stock and bring to a boil over high heat, about 3 minutes. Lower to a simmer and add the basil and sambuca to the pan. Cook for 1 minute to allow the flavors to mingle.

Add the tuna to the pan with the sauce and cook for 1 minute for rare tuna, or longer if you prefer.

Joseph Tucker's Blackening Seasoning Mix

MAKES ABOUT 1 CUP

2 tablespoons ground paprika
2 tablespoons chili powder
1 tablespoon freshly ground black or white
   pepper
1 tablespoon cayenne pepper
1 tablespoon onion powder
1 tablespoon garlic powder
1 tablespoon Old Bay seasoning or other
   seafood seasoning

Mix all the ingredients together and store in an airtight container.

Jamie Shannon's Crawfish Boil

⁓

SERVES 12 GENEROUSLY

We visited New Orleans during Jazz Fest weekend a few years ago and asked Jamie Shannon, the executive chef of Commander's Palace, to cook dinner for us. He prepared a crawfish boil that was positively delicious. Shannon recommends selecting very fresh garlic, which not only contributes important flavor to the boil but also may be eaten itself after it's boiled. He cautions home cooks to add the corn just before the crawfish to make sure the cobs don't get overcooked. If cooking this indoors, keep the exhaust fan on or work near an open window to ensure proper ventilation.

8 cups salt
12 gallons water
1 sack of live crawfish (40 to 45 pounds)
6 cups Creole Seafood Seasoning (page 150)
    or any Creole seasoning mix
2 cups cayenne pepper
2 cups whole black peppercorns
15 bay leaves
12 lemons, halved
12 heads garlic, each head cut in half
10 onions, peeled and quartered
3 pounds small new potatoes, scrubbed, skin on
12 ears corn, shucked and halved

Fill a washtub or ice chest with the water and 2 cups of the salt, stir, and place the crawfish in the mix. As they swim around, the salt will cause them to purge themselves of impurities and cleanse their outer shells. (Let them purge for 30 to 40 minutes; they need to stay alive until you're ready to cook them.

CHEF'S NOTES

Be sure to have a large pot, at least 20 gallons, with a basket and a lid, which helps the boil to boil faster. You'll probably use a propane tank, so be sure to have enough fuel. Also, place the pot on the burner before you add the water or it will be too heavy to lift.

When buying crawfish, make sure they are lively.

This same procedure can be used for crabs or shrimp.

You also can have a lot of fun personalizing your boil by adding sausage, mushrooms, artichokes, etc.

While that's happening, pour the 12 gallons of water into a 20-gallon pot. Add the remaining salt and the seasoning, cayenne pepper, black peppercorns, bay leaves, and lemons. Boil for 15 minutes. Put half the garlic, half the onions, and half the potatoes in a basket insert. Place the basket in the water and cook for 4 to 5 minutes. Add half the corn and return the water to a boil.

Drain the crawfish from their purging water, add half of them to the basket, and bring to a rolling boil. Turn off the heat and let soak for 10 minutes. Pull out the basket, drain, and dump the basket's contents onto a newspaper-lined table. Repeat with the remaining crawfish, garlic, onions, potatoes, and corn.

Serve crawfish, corn, onions, and garlic to each person.

NOTE: You certainly can boil a small amount of crawfish in a smaller vessel, do it indoors, and serve it to a smaller gathering, but in New Orleans, this is for an outdoor bash.

Creole Seafood Seasoning

MAKES ABOUT 2 CUPS

⅓ cup table salt
¼ cup granulated or powdered garlic
¼ cup freshly ground black pepper
2 tablespoons cayenne pepper, or to taste (See Note)
2 tablespoons dried thyme
2 tablespoons dried basil
2 tablespoons dried oregano
⅓ cup dried paprika
3 tablespoons granulated or powdered onion

Thoroughly combine all the ingredients in a blender, food processor, or mixing bowl and pour the mixture into a large glass or plastic jar. Seal it so that it's airtight. It will keep indefinitely.

NOTE: Cayenne pepper is the main source of heat in this mixture. If you wish, reduce the quantity by as much as half.

Poultry

Jim Botsacos's Lemon Garlic Roasted Chicken

SERVES 4

Jim Botsacos, the executive chef of Molyvos restaurant in New York City, refers to the combination of lemon, olive oil, and oregano as the "trinity" of Greek cooking. And he's happy to comply with tradition at his upscale restaurant in midtown Manhattan. At Molyvos, Botsacos pairs the chicken with potatoes that are cooked in the natural juices of the bird. Though very simple, this recipe approximates the one on the menu at the restaurant, where lemons are placed in the chicken cavity and the bird is roasted very slowly and basted with a sauce of lemon juice, olive oil, and oregano.

1 whole chicken, about 4 pounds, ready to cook
Coarse salt and freshly ground black pepper to taste
1 lemon, juiced, seeds discarded, lemon halves reserved
8 cloves garlic, 4 smashed and 4 roughly chopped
3 generous tablespoons roughly chopped flat-leaf parsley leaves, stems reserved
2 medium yellow onions, thinly sliced
6 tablespoons extra-virgin olive oil
5 teaspoons dried oregano leaves
2 tablespoons unsalted butter, melted
4 large Red Bliss potatoes, scrubbed
1 cup chicken stock

Preheat the oven to 400° F.

Rinse the chicken inside and out with cold running water. Drain and pat dry with paper towels. Season with salt and pepper, being sure to season the cavity as well. Stuff the chicken with the lemon halves, 4 smashed cloves garlic, and the parsley stems. Truss the chicken (see box on page 154) and set aside.

Toss the onions with 3 tablespoons of the olive oil and 1½ teaspoons of the oregano. Season with salt and pepper, half the lemon juice, and 2 tablespoons of the chopped parsley. Spread the mixture evenly over the bottom of a roasting pan.

Toss the potatoes with 2 tablespoons of the remaining olive oil and 1½ teaspoons of the remaining oregano. Season with salt and pepper and the remaining lemon juice. Add the potatoes to the roasting pan, distributing

To Truss a Chicken

You will need a piece of butcher's twine, measuring three times the width of the chicken.

Place the chicken on a clean, dry cutting board. Using kitchen shears or a heavy meat cleaver, clip and remove the wing at the second joint from the breast. Discard or save for stock. Place the chicken on the cutting board, breast side up, with the legs and cavity facing you.

Draw the twine underneath the tail end, holding up the ends of the twine evenly with both hands. Wrap the twine around the thighs and tie them together with the tail end. Make a knot.

Now, extend the twine back as you flip the chicken over toward you, and tie another knot around the wings and neck as the twine runs up around the breast. Tie another knot, bringing the wings and breast together.

This should leave you with a neat little chicken package.

them evenly over the onions and taking care not to disturb the onion layer itself.

Combine the remaining 1 tablespoon olive oil with the remaining 2 teaspoons oregano and the melted butter. Season with salt and pepper and combine with the chopped garlic. Gently rub this mixture over the outside of the chicken and place the chicken in the roasting pan. Pour the chicken stock into the pan, place the pan in the middle of the preheated oven, and baste every 15 minutes until done, 1 to 1¼ hours. (Chicken is done when the leg joints are loose and the juices run clear when the meatiest part of the thigh is pierced with a sharp, thin-bladed knife.) Remove the chicken to a carving board, remove lemons

and parsley stems from cavity, and let rest 15 minutes before serving.

Joseph T. Bonanno, Jr.'s Grilled Stuffed Chicken

SERVES 4

Joe Bonanno, a firefighter turned cookbook writer, claims that he had no problem making dinner for four on our budget because "firefighters are notoriously frugal." Be sure to cook this dish is a well-ventilated kitchen, because the chicken will throw a bit of smoke when prepared on a grill pan. Of course, if you have access to an outdoor grill, the chicken may be cooked there.

4 skinless, boneless chicken breast halves
2 tablespoons olive oil
2 red bell peppers, seeded and roughly chopped
10 scallions, white parts only, roughly chopped
4 cloves garlic, roughly chopped
4 ¼-inch-thick slices mozzarella cheese
¼ cup Italian salad dressing

Cut a deep "pocket" into the side of each chicken breast half by inserting a small, sharp knife into the thicker side, in the upper half of the breast.

In a medium-size saucepan, heat the olive oil over moderate heat. Add the red peppers, scallions, and garlic to the pan and sauté until soft, 3 to 5 minutes per side.

Open the pocket in each chicken breast and insert a slice of the mozzarella cheese and some of the red pepper mixture as deeply as possible. Press down firmly to close the flap.

Place the chicken breasts in a shallow dish. Add the salad dressing and toss to coat the chicken.

Heat a cast-iron grill pan over high heat. Add the chicken and cook until the sides begin to turn white, 3 to 5 minutes. Turn the chicken and grill the second side until the chicken is cooked through and the juices run clear, another 3 to 5 minutes.

Michael Lomonaco's Chicken Fricassee

SERVES 4

In explaining the secret to this recipe's success, Michael Lomonaco points out that all chickens are not created equal. A stewing chicken—older and more flavorful than a roasting chicken—is the optimal choice here. However, a 3½- to 4-pound roasting chicken may be substituted if it's easier for you to obtain one. In either case, the best selection would be a free-range organic bird.

1 stewing chicken, about 4 pounds, cut into
    serving portions
Coarse salt and freshly ground black pepper to
    taste
2 tablespoons extra-virgin olive oil
1 tablespoon unsalted butter
½ cup finely diced onions
½ cup finely diced carrots
½ cup finely diced rutabagas or turnips
½ cup diced fresh tomatoes
1½ cups chicken stock, heated
5 tablespoons roughly chopped basil leaves

Season the chicken parts with a generous sprinkling of salt and freshly ground black pepper. Heat the olive oil together with the butter in a 12- to 14-inch flameproof casserole with a lid over medium heat. Add the chicken—without crowding—skin side down and cook slowly to brown the chicken to a golden brown color. Turn the chicken to brown the other side and add the onion, carrots, and rutabaga to caramelize with the chicken. If necessary, cook the chicken in batches and remove all the chicken pieces to begin cooking the vegetables, then return the chicken at the end. Allow the chicken and vegetables to cook together slowly for 5 to 7 minutes. Add the tomatoes to the pan and cook for 5 minutes.

Add the hot chicken stock and let the fricassee simmer slowly over low heat for 30 to 35 minutes, slightly uncovered.

Carefully transfer the chicken to a serving platter. Add 3 tablespoons of the basil to the pan and cook for 2 minutes. Spoon the vegetables around the chicken and pour the excess sauce into a sauceboat. Sprinkle remaining chopped basil leaves over everything and serve.

Lou Piuggi's Moroccan Chicken Tagine with Couscous

SERVES 4

As the executive chef of the Delegates' Dining Room at the United Nations, Lou Piuggi has incorporated influences from the world over into his repertoire. Here, he presents a relatively faithful rendition of a classic Moroccan tagine—named for the Moroccan clay cooking vessel.

If you like, serve this dish with traditional garnishes, such as caramelized onions, raisins, and almonds.

1 chicken, about 3 pounds, cut into 8 pieces
Coarse salt and freshly ground black pepper to taste
3 tablespoons extra-virgin olive oil
½ onion, cut into ¼-inch dice
2 cloves garlic, minced
1 teaspoon ground cumin
1 teaspoon curry powder
1 teaspoon ground cinnamon
1 teaspoon ground coriander
1 teaspoon turmeric
Pinch of saffron threads
Juice of 1 lemon
1 bunch cilantro, stems discarded, roughly chopped
2 cups chicken stock
2 medium zucchini, each cut into 8 slices
1 yellow squash, each cut into 8 slices
2 medium carrots, each cut into 8 slices
2 medium turnips, each cut into 8 slices
Couscous (recipe follows)

Season the chicken pieces with salt and pepper.

In a saucepot big enough to hold the chicken and chicken stock, heat the olive oil over moderate heat. Add the onion, garlic, and spices to the pan and sauté until the onion is soft, 4 to 5 minutes.

Add the lemon juice, cilantro, chicken pieces, and chicken stock to the pan. Raise the heat to high and bring the stock to a boil. Reduce the heat to a simmer, cover, and cook until the chicken is tender, about 45 minutes. Remove the chicken from the pan and add the zucchini, squash, carrots, and turnips. Cook until the vegetables are tender, about 10 minutes. Return the chicken to the pot.

To serve, mound equal portions of the couscous on each of 4 dinner plates. Spoon some chicken and vegetables on top of the couscous and spoon some of the sauce over and around the plate.

Couscous

1¼ *cups water or chicken stock*
1 6-ounce box Moroccan or other couscous
1 6-tablespoon olive oil
1 teaspoon ground cumin
Coarse salt and freshly ground black pepper to
taste

Bring the water to a boil. Stir the remaining ingredients together in a bowl and cover with the boiling water. Cover with plastic wrap and let sit until all the liquid is absorbed, about 15 minutes.

Scott Campbell's Stuffed Chicken Legs with Mushroom Stuffing

SERVES 4

Scott Campbell, the executive chef and owner of Avenue restaurant on New York City's Upper West Side, firmly believes that eating on a shoestring doesn't have to be an exercise in deprivation. He suggests trying to have some fun when cooking something memorable on a budget, as he does here by wrapping mushrooms into a chicken leg.

This recipe is based on one from Avenue's menu that is often complemented with bacon lardons, goat cheese, or walnuts and a hearty Burgundian sauce. But the peasant-food appeal of this dish shines through even in this simplified version.

2 tablespoons unsalted butter

½ onion, cut into ¼-inch dice

8 ounces white button mushroooms, trimmed, wiped clean with a damp cloth or paper towel, and minced (ideally in a food processor)

Coarse salt and freshly ground black pepper to taste

3 tablespoons roughly chopped flat-leaf parsley leaves

4 chicken legs

2 tablespoons canola oil

2 tablespoons water

3 ounces (5 tablespoons) granulated sugar

4 Belgian endives, root ends trimmed and discarded

Preheat the oven to 500° F.

Melt the butter in a small saucepot set over moderate heat. Add the onion and sauté until transparent, about 5 minutes. Add the mushrooms, season with salt and pepper, and cook until the moisture given off by the mushrooms is cooked off, about 6 minutes. Re-move from the heat, stir in 2 tablespoons of the parsley, and set aside to cool.

Meanwhile, bone the chicken legs (reserve bones for stock or discard). Stuff the legs with the mushroom stuffing. Seal in the mix-ture with bamboo skewers or toothpicks and season the chicken legs with salt and pepper.

Heat the oil in an ovenproof 12-inch sauté pan over moderate heat until it starts to smoke. Add the chicken legs to the pan and sear on all sides. Place in the preheated oven and cook until the legs begin to firm up or un-til an instant-read thermometer inserted into the meat reads 160° F, 20 to 30 minutes.

In an ovenproof 12-inch sauté pan, heat the water and sugar over moderate heat until it begins to caramelize, 4 to 5 minutes. Add the endives to the pan and season with salt and pepper. Place the pan in the oven with the chicken and cook for 15 minutes.

To serve, place an endive on each of 4 plates and top with the caramelized sugar. Add 1 roasted chicken leg to each plate and garnish with the remaining 1 tablespoon parsley. Serve immediately.

Terrance Brennan's Chicken Piccata with Cauliflower, Capers, Sage, and Orange

SERVES 4

Terrance Brennan uses a variation on a brown butter sauce to adorn sautéed chicken slices in this recipe, adding orange and cauliflower to the mix. This sauce may also be used to dress veal and pork, because the sage and orange have an affinity with both of those meats. It may also be used with fish, but substitute mint for sage if you choose to do so. When they're in season, you can substitute blood oranges for the navel oranges for a more unusual flavor.

2 tablespoons extra-virgin olive oil
8 2-ounce slices skinless, boneless chicken breasts
All-purpose flour, for coating
4 tablespoons ($^{1}/_{2}$ stick) unsalted butter, at room temperature
2 tablespoons capers, rinsed
2 navel oranges, peeled and sectioned, juice reserved (if substituting another type of orange, be sure to remove the seeds)
1 cup cauliflower florets, blanched
$^{1}/_{2}$ cup small croutons cut from baguette or other fresh bread, brushed with clarified butter and toasted
8 sage leaves, thinly sliced
Coarse salt and freshly ground black pepper to taste

Heat 1 tablespoon of the olive oil in a 12-inch sauté pan over high heat. Coat the chicken with the flour, shaking off the excess. In a single layer, sauté 4 pieces for 45 seconds on the first side, then 30 seconds on the other. Remove and repeat with the remaining oil and chicken. Keep the cooked chicken warm in a slow oven along with 4 plates.

Heat the butter in a 10-inch sauté pan over high heat until it browns. Add the capers, orange sections and juice, cauliflower, croutons, and sage. Add salt and pepper to taste and heat through for 1 minute.

Place 2 pieces of chicken in the center of each of 4 dinner plates. Drizzle the sauce over and around the chicken.

Charlie Palmer's Seared Chicken Breast with Red Onion Vinaigrette

⸺

SERVES 4

The tangy red onion vinaigrette that dresses the chicken in this recipe will haunt your taste buds. When cooking the chicken, be sure to get the pan very hot before adding the chicken to it.

¹/₂ cup plus 1 tablespoon extra-virgin olive oil

1 cup finely diced red onion

1 teaspoon dried thyme

Coarse salt and freshly ground black pepper to taste

2 cups canned unsalted chicken broth, defatted

³/₄ cup red Burgundy

3 plum tomatoes, peeled, seeded, and cut into ¹/₂-inch dice (page 227)

2 cloves garlic, crushed

1 sachet (see box in right-hand column)

3 tablespoons red wine vinegar

2 whole boneless chicken breasts, skin on

1 tablespoon coarsely cracked black pepper

1 tablespoon corn oil

Place 1 tablespoon olive oil in a small sauté pan and warm over moderate heat. When the oil is hot, add the onion to the pan and sauté for 10 minutes until the onion is well browned and caramelized. Stir in the thyme and season with salt and pepper to taste. Remove from the heat and set aside.

> SACHET
>
> *Using a sachet is a convenient way of infusing a liquid with herbaceous flavor while facilitating the removal of the herbs at the end of the cooking process. You may vary the contents of a sachet in other recipes to suit your own taste.*
>
> *1 bunch parsley stems about the width of your little finger*
>
> *10 peppercorns*
>
> *1 teaspoon dried thyme*
>
> *2 bay leaves*
>
> *Tie all ingredients in a cheesecloth bag.*

Combine the broth, wine, tomatoes, garlic, and sachet in a medium saucepan and set over medium-high heat. Bring to a boil. Lower the heat and simmer for about 25 minutes until the liquid is reduced to ¾ cup. Remove from the heat, discard the sachet, and pour the liquid into a heatproof bowl. Allow to cool for 10 minutes. Alternately whisk in ½ cup olive oil and the vinegar until just emulsified. Stir in the caramelized onion. Keep warm in the top half of a double boiler set over simmering water until ready to serve.

Preheat the oven to 375° F.

Split the chicken breasts in half and trim. Generously season with salt to taste and the cracked pepper. Heat the corn oil in a large, ovenproof sauté pan over medium-high heat. When the oil is hot, add the chicken breasts, skin side down, to the pan. Cook for 5 minutes until golden brown. Turn the breasts and transfer the pan to the preheated oven. Roast for 8 to 10 minutes until cooked through and golden brown. Remove from the oven and place on a stovetop burner over low heat. Add the vinaigrette to the pan and baste to coat. When the chicken is well coated, serve the chicken with the vinaigrette spooned on top.

The American Heart Association's Spicy Grilled Chicken

(from The New American Heart Association Cookbook)

SERVES 6

"Most people think of heart-healthy food as boring, bland, and flavorless," laments Carol Richie, the "national volunteer spokesperson" for the *American Heart Association Cookbook*. But this dish is easy to make, packed with flavor, and well within heart-healthy guidelines. Richie explains that one of the cornerstones of a cardiac-friendly diet is avoiding saturated fats. But when the fat is eliminated (or reduced) from a recipe, one must find flavor from another source, which is why the spices are so important here. The zesty and sweet elements in the dish, and the heady aroma of the grilled chicken itself, keep you from missing the salt, a heart *un*friendly ingredient which has been completely omitted.

This grilled chicken makes great

leftovers, perfect for a chicken salad or even reheated for fajitas.

1 small onion, finely chopped
2 to 3 tablespoons fresh lime juice (1 to 2 medium limes)
1½ tablespoons extra-virgin olive oil
1 to 2 tablespoons finely chopped fresh cilantro leaves
1 small clove garlic, crushed, or ¼ teaspoon bottled minced garlic
½ teaspoon chili powder
Freshly ground black pepper to taste
6 boneless, skinless chicken breast halves, about 4 ounces each, trimmed of all visible fat

In an airtight plastic bag, combine all the ingredients except the chicken.

Rinse the chicken and pat dry with paper towels. Place the chicken in the bag with the marinade and turn to coat. Seal and refrigerate for 2 to 3 hours, turning occasionally to distribute the marinade.

Preheat an outdoor grill to medium-high heat or preheat the broiler. Grill or broil the chicken about 6 inches from the heat until no longer pink in the center, 6 to 7 minutes on each side.

Waldy Malouf's Cold Herbed Roast Chicken with Marinated Japanese Pear Tomatoes

SERVES 4

Waldy Malouf prepared this dish as part of a picnic menu on a summer installment of our show. To create a dish that could be prepared in advance and packed up to travel, he cooked an herb-roasted chicken, then let it chill in the refrigerator. But the chicken can also be served hot the first day and any leftovers served chilled the next day.

1 chicken, about 3 pounds
4 tablespoons extra-virgin olive oil
Coarse salt and freshly ground black pepper to taste
2 bay leaves
12 thyme sprigs, 4 sprigs set aside, leaves of remaining sprigs roughly chopped
12 sage sprigs, 4 sprigs set aside, leaves of remaining sprigs roughly chopped
½ pint Japanese pear, tear-drop, or cherry tomatoes, cut in half
¼ cup balsamic vinegar

Preheat the oven to 400° F.

Rub the chicken all over with 1 tablespoon of the olive oil and season inside and out with salt and pepper. Place the bay leaves and the whole thyme and sage sprigs in the cavity of the chicken and truss it (see page 154 for trussing instructions). Rub half the chopped thyme and half the chopped sage into the skin of the chicken.

Place the chicken in a roasting pan and roast in the preheated oven for 45 minutes. Turn the oven off and let the chicken rest in the turned-off oven for an additional 20 to 30 minutes. Remove from the oven and carve the chicken into eight pieces, setting the pieces on a platter. Sprinkle with the remaining herbs. Cover and chill for 3 to 4 hours or overnight.

When ready to serve, toss the tomatoes with the balsamic vinegar and remaining 3 tablespoons olive oil. Season with salt and pepper. Garnish the chilled chicken platter with the tomatoes and serve.

Spinach-Stuffed Chicken Breast with Mushroom Sauce

(adapted from Gourmet *magazine)*

SERVES 4

When Sara Moulton, the executive chef of *Gourmet* magazine, visited our program, she demonstrated this dish for us. While the spinach mixture usually includes fennel seed, it didn't fit our budget here. If you happen to have some in your pantry, however, by all means add a tablespoon or so.

Moulton offers a few shopping tips for this recipe: When buying spinach, seek out bunches with the smallest leaves, which will be the most tender. As for the chicken, beware of liquid in the bottom of the package, which usually indicates that the pieces have been previously frozen. If you know how to butcher a chicken, buying a whole bird is the cheapest way to go; save the remainder in the freezer for another use.

1 whole boneless chicken breast or 2 boneless
   halves, about ¾ to 1 pound total

1½ tablespoons crushed ice

3 tablespoons heavy cream, well chilled

8 ounces fresh spinach leaves, cooked, squeezed
   dry, chopped, and firmly packed to measure
   ¼ cup

¾ teaspoon coarse salt, plus more to taste

¼ teaspoon freshly grated lemon zest

⅛ teaspoon freshly grated nutmeg

⅛ teaspoon freshly ground black pepper, plus
   more to taste

1 tablespoon vegetable oil

1 teaspoon arrowroot dissolved in 1 tablespoon
   water

8 ounces white mushrooms, trimmed, wiped
   clean with a damp cloth or paper towel, and
   thinly sliced

¾ cup canned chicken broth

Arrange the chicken breast, skin side down, on a dry and impeccably clean cutting board. Making sure that the skin is evenly stretched over the breast, cut the breast in half. Remove the fillet strip from each breast and remove the white tendon. Set the breasts aside.

In a food processor, grind the fillet strips to a fine paste. Add the ice and pulse until the ice is absorbed. With the processor motor running, add the cream, spinach, salt, lemon zest, nutmeg, and pepper. Blend the filling well, scraping down the sides to ensure that all the ingredients are thoroughly incorporated.

Place the breast, skin side up, on your work surface. Beginning at the pointed end,

pull the skins back carefully, leaving the thin transparent membranes attached along the side and ensuring that the skin remains attached at the opposite end.

Using a rubber spatula, spread 3 tablespoons of the spinach filling evenly over each breast, smoothing it to cover the breast. Stretch the skin back over each breast, smoothing and stretching it over the filling to cover and seal it. Reserve the remaining spinach filling for another use.

Tightly wrap the breasts separately in plastic wrap and refrigerate for 1 hour. The chicken may be prepared up to this point 24 hours in advance and kept covered and chilled.

Preheat the oven to 400° F.

In a large ovenproof skillet, heat the oil over moderate heat until it is hot but not smoking. Add the chicken, skin side down, to the pan and season with salt and pepper. Sauté the chicken for 1 to 2 minutes until the skin is golden brown. Turn the breast skin side up, cover, and bake in the preheated oven for about 10 minutes.

Transfer the chicken to a clean and dry cutting board, cover loosely with foil, and let the chicken stand for about 5 minutes.

Meanwhile, make the sauce: Stir the arrowroot to be sure it is dissolved.

Pour off all but 1 tablespoon of the chicken fat from the skillet. Add the mushrooms to the skillet and sauté over moderate heat until the liquid they give off is evaporated, 4 to 5 minutes. Add the chicken broth to the skillet, raise the heat, bring to a boil, and cook for 1 minute. Whisk the arrowroot mixture into the mushroom sauce in the pan. Continue to whisk for 1 minute until the sauce is smooth. Remove from the heat, ad-just the seasoning if necessary, and cover to keep warm.

Holding a knife at a 45-degree angle, slice the chicken crosswise and arrange the slices, overlapping them slightly, on 4 warmed din-ner plates. Spoon some of the sauce around the chicken and serve the remaining mush-room sauce on the side in a sauceboat.

John Doherty's Roast Breast and Braised Legs of Chicken with Olive and Lemon Potatoes and String Beans

SERVES 4

Executive chef John Doherty of the Waldorf-Astoria demonstrated the classic combination of roast breast and braised leg of chicken. The recipe was born of necessity because the leg requires significantly more time to cook than the breast.

Chef Doherty makes a variety of potato dishes that are more of a "chunky purée" than mashed potato. The addition of lemon juice, parsley, tomato, and olive oil really brings the flavor of the potatoes alive. These potatoes are highly versatile and especially good with lamb.

1 3½-pound chicken, washed and patted dry
2 tablespoons unsalted butter
Coarse salt and freshly ground black pepper
½ onion, cut into ¼-inch dice
Juice of 1 lemon
2 cups chicken broth or water

Preheat the oven to 425° F.

Rub the chicken with the butter and season with salt and pepper, being sure to season the cavity as well.

Sprinkle the onion on the bottom of a small roasting pan and place the seasoned chicken on top. Roast the chicken in the preheated oven for 25 minutes. Turn the oven temperature down to 350° F and roast for 30 minutes longer until the juices from the breast run clear when the breast is poked with a sharp, thin-bladed knife.

Remove the chicken from the oven and, with a knife and fork, remove the drumsticks and the thighs. Return the drumsticks and thighs to the roasting pan and add the lemon juice and enough chicken broth to cover the meat halfway. Place the pan back in the oven and bake for 30 minutes, basting every 6 minutes. Remove from the oven.

To serve, slice the breast meat and arrange on a platter around the thigh and leg meat. Pour the cooking juices from the roasting pan through a strainer. Adjust the seasoning and serve as a sauce with the chicken.

Olive and Lemon Potatoes

2 pounds Yukon Gold or Idaho potatoes, scrubbed clean and dried
5 Gaeta olives, pitted and chopped
Juice of 1 lemon
½ bunch flat-leaf parsley, chopped
3 tablespoons unsalted butter
John Doherty's Oven-Dried Tomatoes (recipe follows)
Coarse salt and freshly ground black pepper to taste

Preheat the oven to 375° F.

Bake the potatoes in the preheated oven for 1 hour. Let stand until cool enough to handle. Peel the potatoes and mash with a fork. Stir in the remaining ingredients. Adjust the seasoning and serve hot.

String Beans

8 ounces string beans, cleaned, tips removed
1 tablespoon unsalted butter
Coarse salt and freshly ground black pepper to taste

Boil the beans in boiling salted water for about 5 minutes until just al dente. Drain and toss with the butter. Season with salt and pepper and serve immediately.

JOHN DOHERTY'S OVEN-DRIED TOMATOES

3 plum tomatoes, washed and dried

2 tablespoons extra-virgin olive oil

Coarse salt and freshly ground black pepper to taste

Preheat the oven to 250° F.

Cut the tomatoes in half. Toss with the olive oil and season with salt and pepper. Place the tomatoes, cut side down, on a baking sheet and cook in the preheated oven for 4 to 5 hours until they dry and shrink to half their original size. Remove from the oven, remove the skins, let cool, and chop.

Alfonso Contrisciani's Pepper-Crusted Turkey "London Broil" with Mushroom Confit

SERVES 4

Naming this recipe a "London broil" is more of a nod to its comfort-food style and accompaniments than to the actual cooking method. The turkey breast is gently pounded, seared in a hot pan to caramelize the meat and lock in its juices, and then roasted (not broiled) in a hot oven. The rich pan sauce—containing brandy, Chardonnay, and butter—may seem more suited to flank steak but works very well with the turkey here because of the way the bird is seasoned and seared.

You won't find Pepper-Crusted Turkey "London Broil" on the menu at Philadelphia's Circa restaurant (in fact, you won't find Contrisciani there anymore either); Contrisciani created this variation on the American home-cooking classic for "Chef on a Shoestring." But it is based on the style of Circa's menu, which features many dishes cooked in a wood-burning oven. When Contrisciani cooked there, the mushroom confit was part of Circa's repertoire, where its concentrated woodsy flavor often complemented a filet of beef.

Please note that in order for this recipe to meet its shoestring guidelines, the chef has assumed that you have white wine and Marsala on hand.

1 pound turkey breast, butterflied (cut open from end to end)
4 tablespoons extra-virgin olive oil
1 tablespoon seasoned salt (see Note)
Freshly ground black pepper to taste
1 pound assorted wild mushrooms, such as shiitake, oysters, chanterelles, and hedgehogs, trimmed and wiped clean with a damp cloth or paper towel
1 clove garlic, minced
1 shallot, minced
¼ teaspoon fresh thyme leaves
3 tablespoons brandy
¼ cup Chardonnay or other dry white wine
¼ cup Marsala or Madeira wine
1 tablespoon unsalted butter
Coarse salt to taste
Alfonso Contrisciani's Sweet Potato Gnocchi, freshly cooked (page 103)
1 tablespoon roughly chopped flat-leaf parsley leaves

Preheat the oven to 325° F.

Place the turkey breast between 2 pieces of plastic wrap and beat gently with a meat tenderizer to a thickness of ¼ inch. (If you don't have a tenderizer, use another object such as the bottom of a heavy-bottomed pan or skillet.) Remove the plastic wrap and season the turkey well with 2 tablespoons of the olive oil, seasoned salt, and pepper.

In a heavy-bottomed skillet, heat the remaining olive oil until almost smoking. Add the turkey breast to the pan and sear it, turning often to keep it from scorching, until both sides are lightly browned, about 3 to 4 minutes per side. Transfer to a baking pan with a rack and roast in the preheated oven for 10 to 12 minutes until the internal temperature reaches 160° F. Remove from the heat and keep warm.

Add the mushrooms to the skillet and cook until they begin to give off their liquid, about 2 minutes. Add the garlic and shallot to the skillet and sauté for 2 to 3 more minutes. Add the thyme leaves and flambé with brandy, tilting the skillet away from yourself in case it flares up. Add the Chardonnay and simmer the mushrooms for 12 to 15 minutes over a very low flame, stirring occasionally.

Whisk in the Marsala wine and, finally, the butter. Season to taste with salt and pepper.

Slice the turkey on a diagonal. Divide the gnocchi among 4 dinner plates and top with slices of turkey and mushroom confit. Sprinkle chopped parsley over each serving and serve immediately.

NOTE: Seasoned salt is 2 teaspoons coarse salt, 1 teaspoons ground white pepper, ¼ teaspoon onion powder, and ¼ teaspoon garlic powder.

Ray Arpke's Turkey Breast Scaloppine with Mushrooms and Mustard Butter Sauce

SERVES 4

This may sound like a shoestring recipe in which a resourceful chef substituted turkey for veal, but turkey is actually one of the classic scaloppine meats. Usually, a sauce must be created from scratch for a scaloppine because the cooking method doesn't yield enough juices for a classic pan sauce. Chef Ray Arpke, of Florida's Euphemia Haye restaurant, does a fine job of providing one here making economical use of the turkey trimmings in the base.

2½ pounds turkey breast, skin and bones removed and reserved
½ cup sliced onion (reserve ends and skins)
1 bay leaf
Pinch of thyme leaves
6 black peppercorns
1 tablespoon minced onion
½ cup all-purpose flour
8 tablespoons (1 stick) unsalted butter, at room temperature
2 teaspoons grainy mustard
Coarse salt and freshly ground black pepper to taste
4 ounces white mushrooms, thinly sliced

Using a sharp knife and a steady hand, slice the turkey breast into 12 thin slices of uniform thickness. Remove any tendons or connective tissue and reserve it with the skin and bones. One at a time, place the turkey breast slices between 2 pieces of plastic wrap and pound gently with a meat mallet to form 12 individual medallions. (If you don't have a mallet, use a rolling pin or a heavy-bottomed pan or pot.) Lay the medallions out on a plate, cover with plastic wrap, and refrigerate.

Begin a stock by browning the turkey skin and bones and onion ends and skins in a 2-quart saucepot over moderate heat. Add enough water to the saucepot to cover the contents. Add the bay leaf, thyme, and peppercorns to the pot and bring the water to a boil. Lower the heat and simmer the stock slowly for 2 hours. Skim the fat from the top of the stock as it gathers, reserving the fat as you go. Cook until the stock is reduced to 1 cup. Strain and reserve.

In a saucepot, sauté the minced onion in 1 tablespoon of the reserved turkey fat over moderate heat for 1 minute. Add 1 tablespoon of the flour and cook for 1 to 2 minutes. Whisk in the turkey stock. Simmer for 3 to 4 minutes to cook out the flour taste. Gradually whisk in 6 tablespoons of the butter to form a rich emulsion, then whisk in the grainy mustard. Reserve sauce.

Melt 2 tablespoons of the remaining but-

ter in a large sauté pan over moderate heat. Season the turkey medallions with salt and pepper and coat them with the remaining flour. Shake off the excess flour and sauté them. When the butter begins to brown, turn the medallions over and add the sliced onion and mushrooms to the pan. Sauté until the turkey is cooked through and the vegetables are cooked. (You may have to do this in 2 or 3 batches.)

Arrange the medallions on a serving platter and top with the mustard butter sauce.

Meats

Erik Blauberg's "Blau-burger"

2 pounds ground sirloin or beef
¼ cup duck fat, or 2 tablespoons vegetable shortening, at room temperature
1 teaspoon ground fennel
½ teaspoon cayenne pepper
½ teaspoon ground black pepper
1 teaspoon fresh thyme leaves
½ teaspoon chopped fresh rosemary leaves
1 large egg
¼ cup minced onion

SERVES 4

In the long and illustrious history of the '21' Club, each chef has contributed his or her own variation on the most famous burger in America. Erik Blauberg's burger has earned praise as high as any other chef's, inspiring *Esquire*'s John Mariani to name it the "best burger in America." Though he has been asked for the recipe numerous times, Blauberg has only divulged it once—on "Chef on a Shoestring."

It may not sound romantic, but the secret of this burger may be summed up in two words: duck fat. Because it has a lower melting point than other fats, duck fat keeps the burger juicy once the patty has been seared in a pan. Purchase duck fat from your butcher, but plan ahead—he or she may need to special order it for you.

Preheat a grill or broiler.

In a stainless-steel mixing bowl, combine the beef, fat, fennel, cayenne, black pepper, thyme, rosemary, egg, and onion. Using your hands, knead until all ingredients are incorporated evenly.

Divide the beef mixture into 4 8-ounce burgers. Pack and shape them tightly.

Place the burgers on the hot grill or under the broiler and cook for approximately 4½ minutes on each side for a medium-rare burger. Cook longer if a more well-done burger is desired.

Serve on a bun with potatoes, such as those on pages 200 or 202, and/or Erik Blauberg's Pickled Vegetables (page 198).

Michael Lomonaco's Chile-Rubbed Beef Pot Roast

MAKES 6 TO 8 SERVINGS

This recipe illustrates the taste benefits of beef with a high fat marbleization, which creates a wonderful, juicy effect when cooked. As for the chili powder in this dish, Lomonaco prefers powdered ancho chiles to the generic variety. For those seeking an authentic Southwestern smokiness, add a can of chipotle chilies in adobo sauce.

1 tablespoon ground cumin
1 tablespoon ground coriander
1 tablespoon chili powder
1½ teaspoons cayenne pepper
1 teaspoon coarse salt
1 tablespoon freshly ground black pepper
1 3-pound beef chuck roast
2 tablespoons extra-virgin olive oil
2 carrots, peeled and chopped
1 large onion, roughly chopped
2 cloves garlic, finely chopped
2 celery stalks, roughly chopped
½ cup roughly chopped plum tomatoes
1½ cups beef broth, plus more if needed

Preheat the oven to 350° F.

Combine the cumin, coriander, chili powder, cayenne, salt, and pepper in a bowl and rub the spice mix into the beef.

Heat the olive oil in a large ovenproof skillet over medium heat. Place the spice-rubbed beef in the skillet and sear both sides well. Add the carrots, onion, garlic, and celery and cook for 5 to 6 minutes. Add the tomatoes and beef broth and place a tight-fitting lid on the skillet.

Place the roast in the oven and slowly cook for 1 hour. Turn the beef and cook for ½ hour more before removing from the oven. Test for doneness by inserting a knife to feel for tenderness. Continue to cook with the lid tightly in place for any additional time if necessary. Add more beef broth or water if the liquid doesn't rise halfway up the side of the beef at all times.

Remove the pot roast from the oven and

carefully spoon off and discard any fat. Allow the beef to rest for 20 minutes before serving.

Serve with accompaniments such as Ira Freehof's Roast Garlic Mashed Potatoes (page 200) or John Schenk's Yukon Gold Potato and Horseradish Salad (page 202).

Thomas Salamunovich's Lamb with Slow-Roasted Vegetables

SERVES 4

In this hearty dish, slowly roasted tomatoes are matched with roasted potatoes. Both vegetables pair very well with the aromatic rub that seasons the lamb. Chef Salamunovich used a lamb shoulder that has a gamy quality.

4 Roma tomatoes, peeled and cut in half
    lengthwise

4 tablespoons olive oil

1 head garlic (about 20 cloves), peeled and
    puréed in a food processor

Coarse salt and freshly ground black pepper to
    taste

8 small new potatoes or baby Yukon Golds,
    halved

1 large zucchini cut into ½-inch dice

1 cup dried bread crumbs

1 bunch flat-leaf parsley, stems removed, leaves
    roughly chopped

1 18-ounce boneless lamb shoulder, tied (ask
    your butcher to do this)

3 tablespoons canola oil

1 cup water

¼ cup balsamic vinegar

½ cup Niçoise olives, pitted and roughly
    chopped

The night before the day you plan to serve this dish, preheat the oven to 200° F. Toss the tomatoes with 2 tablespoons of the olive oil and a pinch of the puréed garlic and season with salt and pepper. Spread out the tomatoes, cut side up, on a sheet pan and roast in the oven for 12 hours.

About 1 hour before serving this dish, preheat the oven to 300° F. If the tomatoes are still cooking, raise the oven heat.

Toss the potatoes with the remaining 2 tablespoons olive oil in a roasting pan and season with salt and pepper. Roast in the preheated oven until golden brown and soft, about 1 hour. During the last 10 minutes,

add the zucchini to the roasting pan and toss them to coat lightly with olive oil and seasoning. When fully cooked, remove the potatoes and zucchini and keep warm. Remove the tomatoes when they are done and keep warm separately. Do not turn off the oven, but increase the temperature to 375° F.

Meanwhile, purée the remaining garlic, the bread crumbs, and half the chopped parsley into a paste. Season the lamb liberally with salt and pepper, pressing the seasoning into the meat. In an ovenproof skillet or sauté pan, heat the canola oil over high heat. Add the lamb to the pan and sear on all sides, about 4 minutes total. Transfer the lamb to a clean, dry surface and rub the herb paste all over the lamb. Place the lamb in a roasting pan and cook in the preheated oven for 35 minutes until an instant-read thermometer inserted into the center of the lamb reads 135° F.

When the lamb is done, remove it from the oven and transfer the lamb to a rack, keeping it warm by tenting with foil. Pour off any grease in the pan and add the water and balsamic vinegar to the pan. Place the roasting pan over high heat and cook until the liquid is reduced by half, about 5 minutes, whisking to combine the liquids and loosen any bits that are stuck to the bottom of the pan. Add the olives to the pan, season with salt and pepper, remove from the heat, and keep warm.

To serve, decoratively arrange the tomatoes, potatoes, and zucchini around the perimeter of a serving platter. Untie the lamb, cut it into 4 round slices, and place them overlapping in the center of the platter. Spoon the sauce over and around the lamb and finish with the remaining chopped parsley. Serve immediately, passing any extra sauce on the side.

John Villa's Thai Pork "Dumplings"

SERVES 4 TO 6

These Thai-inspired "dumplings" are more like pork patties and make a substantial main course, offset by crunchy, tangy pickled cucumbers. When shopping for pork, look for an appealing rosy color and good marbleization. For the scallops, seek out those that are shiny and opaque but not too white. You may substitute regular white rice for jasmine rice here, but the latter has a stickiness that suits this recipe very well.

FOR THE PICKLED CUCUMBER:

1 cucumber, seeded, peeled, and cut into 1/4-inch dice

1 cup rice vinegar

1/2 teaspoon hot red pepper flakes

1 tablespoon sugar

1 tablespoon coarse salt, plus more to taste

1 carrot, peeled and cut into julienne

For the "dumplings":

1½ pounds ground pork

1 teaspoon finely chopped ginger

Grated zest of ½ lime

1 sprig cilantro, chopped

2 tablespoons Thai fish sauce (available in specialty markets and the Asian section of well-stocked grocery stores)

1 cup cooked Thai jasmine or regular long-grain white rice

3 tablespoons canola oil

3 ounces medium-sized scallops

Freshly ground black pepper to taste

TO MAKE THE PICKLED CUCUMBER:

Mix the cucumber, rice vinegar, pepper flakes, sugar, salt, and carrot. Refrigerate for at least 4 hours. (Before serving, remove from the refrigerator and allow to come up to room temperature while preparing the remainder of the dish.)

TO MAKE THE DUMPLINGS:

In a mixing bowl, combine the pork, ginger, lime zest, cilantro, fish sauce, and cooked rice. Stir to combine well. Form into 4 small ½-inch-thick patties. Refrigerate for 1 hour.

Preheat the oven to 350° F.

In an ovenproof sauté pan, warm 2 tablespoons of the canola oil over moderate heat. Add the "dumplings" to the pan and brown them for 2 to 3 minutes, turning them to avoid scorching. Place the sauté pan in the preheated oven and cook the dumplings for 4 minutes.

Meanwhile, heat the remaining 1 tablespoon canola oil in a sauté pan over moderate heat. Add the scallops to the pan and sauté for about 1 minute on each side until both sides are lightly browned. Season with salt and pepper.

Place 1 "dumpling" on each of 4 warmed dinner plates. Divide the scallops and pickled cucumbers evenly among the plates. Serve immediately.

Matthew Lake's Grilled Pork Chops with Black Bean Salsa, Grilled Sweet Potatoes, and Roasted Corn

⁓

SERVES 4

This colorful Southwestern dish was created by Matthew Lake for a summertime segment on which we asked him to cook dinner for four on an outdoor grill. Lake made prominent use of corn and tomatoes, both at the height of their season (and affordability) in the late summer. Sweet potatoes, usually considered a food of the fall, are grilled in slices and feel right at home in this warm-weather context. Not only does their flavor round out this ensemble, but their vibrant orange provides a welcome burst of color on the plate.

Since most of the components in this dish are cooked on the grill, set yourself up for success by making sure the grate is well brushed, lightly oiled, and good and hot before using it. You'll be warming the components of this recipe in stages, so also pay close attention to keeping the grate well oiled throughout the process. Chef Lake offers the following technique for doing this: Roll a towel into a small bundle and tie it tightly with butcher twine. Dip the towel itself in oil and keep it close by while grilling. When your grill needs greasing, manipulate the towel with tongs and use it to oil the grate; the tongs will enable you to stay far enough from the flame to avoid getting burned by a flare-up should one occur.

FOR THE SALSA:
2 vine-ripened tomatoes, peeled, seeded, and cut into ¼-inch dice
2 cups cooked black beans, drained and well rinsed
1 medium onion, cut into ¼-inch dice
1 jalapeño pepper, seeded and minced
Juice of 1 lime
4 sprigs basil, stems removed, roughly chopped
Coarse salt to taste

TO MAKE THE SALSA:
Combine the tomatoes, black beans, onion, jalapeño, and lime juice in a mixing bowl. Add half the basil and season with salt. Mix well and refrigerate for at least ½ hour before serving.

FOR THE CORN:

4 ears yellow corn, husks intact but silk removed

1 tablespoon unsalted butter (approximately)

Coarse salt and freshly ground black pepper to
taste

4 sprigs basil, stems removed, roughly chopped

TO PREPARE THE CORN:

Peel back the husks on the corn. Rub each ear
with a little butter and season with salt, pepper, and some of the chopped basil. Pull the
husks back over the corn.

*FOR THE SWEET POTATO,
PORK CHOPS, AND
ASSEMBLY:*

1 medium sweet potato, well washed and cut
into ¼-inch slices

2 tablespoons vegetable oil (approximately)

Coarse salt and freshly ground black pepper to
taste

4 6-ounce boneless pork chops

2 tablespoons unsalted butter

Prepare an outdoor grill and let the coals
burn until covered with white ash.

Drizzle each potato slice with a little vegetable oil, then season on both sides with salt
and pepper.

Lightly oil the pork on both sides with
some vegetable oil, then season on both sides
with salt and pepper.

Bank the hot coals on one side of the grill.
Place the corn on the hot side of the grill and
cook, rotating often, for 3 to 4 minutes. Remove to the other side of the grill to keep

warm over the indirect heat. Add the sweet
potato slices to the grill and cook for 2 minutes on each side. Remove to the other side of
the grill to keep warm with the corn. Add the
pork chops to the grill and cook until heated
through, 15 to 20 minutes, depending on the
thickness of the pork chops and heat of the
grill.

Place a pork chop in the center of each of
4 dinner plates. Fan the grilled sweet potatoes
around one side of the pork. Place an ear of
corn on each plate and top the pork with the
salsa. Serve immediately.

Matt Reichel's Berghoff's Pepper Steak

SERVES 4

When Matt Reichel took the helm at the Berghoff restaurant in Chicago, he adjusted their classic pepper steak recipe to keep the peppers crisp-tender and preserve their flavor and crunch.

1 20-ounce flank steak, cut on the diagonal into ¼-inch-thick slices
Coarse salt and freshly ground black pepper to taste
2 tablespoons vegetable oil
1 yellow bell pepper, seeded and julienned
1 red bell pepper, seeded and julienned
1 green bell pepper, seeded and julienned
1 cup beef stock or water

Preheat the broiler or prepare an outdoor grill and let burn until the coals are covered with white ash.

Rub the flank steak slices with salt and coarsely ground black pepper. Place the seasoned steak on the grill or under the broiler and cook approximately 1 minute on each side. Remove the steak from the grill or broiler and keep warm.

Heat the oil in a sauté pan. Add the peppers and stock to the pan and cook the peppers until just soft, about 5 minutes, leaving the peppers al dente so they retain their bright color. Season with salt and pepper.

Mix the grilled steak with the peppers and cook all the ingredients until heated through, 2 to 3 minutes. Divide the peppers and steak evenly among 4 dinner plates and serve.

Ira Freehof's Meatloaf

SERVES 4

Five years before opening his first Comfort Diner, Ira Freehof tasted the most incredible meatloaf he had ever experienced. Though he steadfastly refuses to identify the source, he persuaded the person who cooked it for him to share the recipe, then tucked it away and patiently waited to unleash it on the New York City dining population. When he did, in 1996, it met with peerless praise, such as that from *Gourmet* magazine's David Rosengarten, who called it "devastatingly delicious." Among its tricks are the inclusion of pork and the use of oatmeal instead of bread crumbs to retain as much moisture as possible.

1 pound ground beef, 80% lean
4 ounces ground veal
4 ounces ground pork
(Note: A "meatloaf variety" pack of beef, pork, and veal may be used.)
2 large eggs, at room temperature
3/4 cup milk
1/2 cup oatmeal
1/2 cup canned peeled tomatoes, drained and roughly chopped
1/3 cup finely diced celery
1/2 cup finely diced onion
1 clove garlic, minced
1 tablespoon dried basil
1 tablespoon dried thyme
1 tablespoon dried oregano
1 teaspoon coarse salt
1 teaspoon freshly ground black pepper
Mushroom Gravy (recipe follows)

Preheat the oven to 425° F.

In a large bowl thoroughly combine the beef, pork, and veal. In a separate bowl, beat the eggs, then stir in the milk and oats. Pour the egg mixture into the meat mixture and combine thoroughly. Add the remaining ingredients and combine again until fully incorporated. Form into a loaf in a roasting pan and bake for 45 to 50 minutes. Remove to a platter and keep warm while making the mushroom gravy. (Note: Be sure to reserve ½ cup drippings for the gravy.) Serve with Ira Freehof's Shredded Zucchini (page 199) and Roast Garlic Mashed Potatoes (page 200).

Mushroom Gravy

1½ cups water
½ cup drippings from the meatloaf
¼ cup all-purpose flour
4 large button mushrooms, thinly sliced
Coarse salt and freshly ground black pepper to
    taste

Pour the water into the meatloaf's roasting pan and stir and scrape with a wooden spoon or whisk to loosen the browned bits at the bottom.

Pour the reserved meatloaf drippings into a 2-quart saucepan and warm over medium heat. Gradually stir in the flour until smooth. Add the sliced mushrooms and cook, stirring constantly, until mixture is slightly browned, 4 to 5 minutes. Slowly stir in the liquid from the roasting pan and cook, stirring, until thickened. Season with salt and pepper to taste.

Michael Lomonaco's Marinated and Grilled Pork Medallions

SERVES 6 TO 8

Michael Lomonaco served this dish as part of a tailgate menu to demonstrate the versatility of the outdoor grill, although the recipe may also be prepared on a cast-iron grill pan. While most people think of hot dogs and hamburgers as the requisite grill fare, Michael encourages them to open their minds to other possibilities, in this case marinated pork medallions. "They cook just as quickly," he says, "and they're just as easy to prepare."

Michael employs Asian flavors to add a fruity tang to the pork here. This recipe is also extremely versatile; you can make a sandwich of the pork and grilled vegetables on country bread or Portuguese-style rolls. Serve Michael Lomonaco's Quince Fruit Mustard (page 195) on the side. You can grill the vegetables a day in advance and reheat them for service.

1 3-pound pork loin
1 cup apple cider
$^1/_4$ cup soy sauce
$^1/_4$ cup honey
2 tablespoons ketchup
$^1/_2$ teaspoon ground ginger
2 red bell peppers, seeded and cut into wedges
2 green bell peppers, seeded and cut into wedges
2 large onions, cut into wedges and skewered
$^1/_4$ cup vegetable oil
Coarse salt and freshly ground black pepper to
    taste

Cut the pork loin into ½-inch-thick medallions. Combine the cider, soy, honey, ketchup, and ginger in a bowl. Place the pork medallions in a large, flat dish and pour the cider mixture over them. Cover and let the pork marinate for at least 2 hours or overnight in the refrigerator.

Heat an outdoor grill until hot. When ready to grill, brush the vegetables with oil, and season to taste with salt and pepper. Place on the grill and grill for about 8 minutes. Remove the pork from the marinade and drain for a moment. Season the pork to taste with salt and pepper and grill 3 to 4 minutes on each side over high heat to coincide with the end of the vegetable cooking time. (Watch the medallions closely; they will cook quickly because they are thinly sliced.) Be sure that the pork's juices run clear when removed from the grill. If they do not, return to the grill and cook for another 30 seconds or so on each side.

John Schenk's Chile-Rubbed London Broil with Barbecued Onions

SERVES 4

In this recipe, John Schenk jazzes up a traditional London broil, first marinating it in dark beer, then seasoning it with tantalizing spices. The result is a far cry from the memories of bland meat most of us retain from childhood. The addition of barbecued onions to the plate only increases the succulence of this dish.

$1^2/_3$-pound London broil
1 bottle dark beer
$^1/_3$ cup chili powder, preferably a high-quality
    brand such as De Choix
1 teaspoon dried thyme or basil leaves
1 teaspoon freshly ground black pepper
Coarse salt to taste
2 tablespoons canola oil
John Schenk's Barbecued Onions (page 202)

Place the London broil in a shallow dish and pour the beer over it. Cover with plastic wrap and marinate overnight in the refrigerator.

When ready to prepare the London broil, preheat the oven to 425° F.

Remove the meat from the beer marinade and pat dry with paper towels. In a small bowl, combine the chili powder, thyme, and black pepper. Coat the meat with the seasonings, then season with salt as well.

Warm the oil in an ovenproof sauté pan over medium heat. Add the meat and brown it on all sides. Place the sauté pan in the preheated oven and cook for 5 to 6 minutes depending on the thickness of the London broil and desired doneness. Remove the sauté pan from oven, remove the meat from the pan, and let the meat rest for 4 minutes.

Meanwhile, gently reheat the barbecued onions. Thinly slice the London broil across the grain and place the slices on a platter. Spoon the barbecued onions over the meat. Serve immediately.

Mario Batali's Pork Scaloppine

SERVES 4

Frequent "Chef on a Shoestring" guest Mario Batali turns to the Italian college town of Perugia for his inspiration in this recipe. Pork scallopine is a popular dish in student trattorias because pork—much of which is raised in Montalcino and Assisi—is less expensive than beef. This dish can be found in restaurants catering to Italian students for the equivalent of eight U.S. dollars.

$1/4$ cup extra-virgin olive oil
$1/2$ cup all-purpose flour
Coarse salt and freshly ground black pepper to taste
4 scallops boneless pork loin, 1 inch thick
4 ounces prosciutto, cut into $1/4$-inch strips
2 cloves garlic, thinly sliced
2 tablespoons capers, rinsed and drained
$1/2$ cup white wine
4 anchovy fillets, rinsed and chopped
Grated zest of 2 lemons
6 sage leaves
1 cup lentils, cooked and kept warm

In a 12- to 14-inch sauté pan, heat the olive oil over medium-high heat until smoking. Season the flour with salt and pepper. Coat the pork pieces with the seasoned flour and shake off the excess. Add the pork to the pan and sauté until golden brown on one side, about 5 to 6 minutes. Remove the pork from the pan and hold briefly on a clean, dry surface or plate. Add the prosciutto, garlic, and capers to the pan and cook for 2 minutes. Add the wine, anchovies, lemon zest, and sage to the pan. Stir well, then return the pork to the pan, turning it over to cook the other side. Cook until heated through and the liquid is reduced by half, 8 to 10 minutes.

Place the pork pieces on a warm plate, cover with spoonfuls of sauce, and serve with the warm lentils.

Aaron Bashy's Pork Spareribs with Polenta

SERVES 4

Aaron Bashy offers two crucial bits of advice to home cooks making this dish: Let the ribs marinate a long time before cooking, and be sure to stir the polenta constantly, keeping it at a very low simmer to keep it from spraying out of the pot.

1¼ pounds pork spareribs, separated into
    individual ribs (ask your butcher to do this)
6 tablespoons red wine vinegar
1 tablespoon honey
2 cloves garlic, crushed
½ teaspoon Dijon mustard
Coarse salt and freshly ground black pepper to
    taste
2 cups heavy cream
2 cups water
1 cup polenta or coarse cornmeal

In a bowl large enough to hold the ribs, combine the vinegar, honey, garlic, and mustard and season with salt and pepper. Add the ribs to the bowl, toss to coat thoroughly with the

mixture, and marinate, covered in the refrigerator, for at least 8 hours.

Preheat the oven to 400° F.

Remove the ribs from the marinade and place on a baking sheet. Bake for 20 minutes in the preheated oven, then lower the heat to 350° F and continue cooking for an additional 40 minutes until the meat falls easily away from the bone.

In a medium-size saucepan, heat the cream and water over moderate heat to a boil. Gradually whisk in the polenta. (Do this as soon as the liquid boils to ensure that it doesn't boil over.) Continue whisking the polenta for 2 to 4 minutes after all liquid has been absorbed, about 10 to 12 minutes total cooking time. Season with salt and pepper. Cover and keep warm in a double boiler until the spareribs are ready or—better yet—time the cooking to coincide with spareribs' finishing time.

To serve, ladle the polenta into each of 4 wide bowls. Top with equal amounts of spareribs and serve.

Peter Kelly's Roasted Rack of Pork, Butternut Squash Purée, and Julienned Apples

SERVES 4

Chef and restaurateur Peter Kelly makes this dish at his upstate New York restaurants, where he sauces it with a port reduction. The key to cooking it successfully is to avoid "incinerating the pork—just cook it until the juices run clear."

1 2-pound butternut squash

1 teaspoon ground cinnamon

1 teaspoon ground nutmeg

1 teaspoon ground cloves

Coarse salt and freshly ground black pepper to
    taste

1 tablespoon unsalted butter

1 4-rib rack of pork, trimmed and bones
    frenched (ask your butcher to do this)

1 clove garlic, chopped

1 tablespoon extra-virgin olive oil

2 Cortland apples

Juice of ½ lemon

Preheat the oven to 375° F.

Halve the butternut squash lengthwise and remove the seeds. Sprinkle the inside of both halves with the cinnamon, nutmeg, and cloves and season with salt and pepper. Place the squash, cut sides down, on a baking sheet. Reserve.

Rub the pork with the chopped garlic and season with salt and pepper. In an ovenproof skillet large enough to hold the pork, heat the oil over moderate heat until very hot. Place the pork in the skillet and sear on all sides, about 1 minute per side. Turn the pork bone side up and place the skillet in the oven. Roast for 45 to 60 minutes until the juices run clear. Remove from the oven and let rest for 15 to 20 minutes.

Meanwhile, place the squash, on its baking sheet, in the oven as well. Bake until very soft, about 1 hour. Remove from the oven and scoop out the squash flesh from the shells. Discard the shells.

In a food processor, purée the squash with the butter until smooth. Season with salt and pepper. Set aside and keep warm.

Meanwhile, core the apples and cut into julienne strips. Toss with the lemon juice to keep the apples from turning brown.

To serve, place a generous spoonful of butternut squash purée in the center of each of 4 warmed dinner plates. Slice the roast into 4 chops and set 1 on each mound of purée. Sprinkle the julienned apples around the plates. Serve immediately.

Linda West Eckhardt's Beef and Tomato Stir-Fry with Whiskey and Black Bean Sauce

(adapted from Stylish One-Dish Dinners)

⌒

SERVES 6

This stir-fried Cantonese dish from seasoned cookbook author Linda West Eckhardt is (like most Cantonese cooking) meant to be eaten as soon as it comes out of the wok, but it also makes for sensational leftovers the next day. When cooking it, be sure that the wok is thoroughly preheated to prevent the food from sticking, and add the ingredients one layer at a time, stirring constantly to ensure that they are warmed through as quickly as possible.

If you choose to use ready-made black bean sauce, taste for salt before seasoning the dish because prepared sauces can be quite salty. You may cook the rice while the steak is marinating.

FOR THE MARINADE AND STEAK:
2 tablespoons coarse salt
1 tablespoon soy sauce
1 teaspoon whiskey
1 teaspoon cornstarch
2 tablespoons peanut oil
1 pound lean flank steak, cut into thin slices across the grain

FOR THE SAUCE:
1 tablespoon dried salted black-beans, or 2 tablespoons Chinese-style black-bean garlic sauce
2 cloves garlic, crushed (omit if using black bean sauce)
3 tablespoons water (omit if using black bean sauce)

3 tablespoons peanut oil
1 scallion with top, minced
6 medium plum tomatoes (about 1½ pounds), cored and quartered
1½ teaspoons sugar
½ cup chicken broth
1 tablespoon oyster sauce
4 cups cooked white rice

Special equipment: a large wok

In a medium bowl, combine the marinade ingredients. Add the flank steak and rub the mixture into the meat with your fingers. Cover and set aside to marinate for 20 minutes.

If you're using prepared black bean sauce, skip this step: While the steak is marinating, mash the black beans and the garlic together in a bowl with a spoon. Stir in the water and set aside.

Heat a wok over medium-high heat and add 2 tablespoons of the oil. Add the scallion and stir-fry for about 30 seconds. Add the black bean sauce and stir-fry for about 15 seconds. Add the meat and cook, stirring, until it begins to lose its pink color, 2 to 3 minutes. Transfer the meat to a bowl and set aside.

Add the remaining 1 tablespoon oil to the wok and heat. Add the tomatoes and stir-fry just until they begin to lose their shape, 1 to 2 minutes, sprinkling them with the sugar to hasten their browning. Add the broth, cover the wok, and continue cooking until the tomatoes are thickened, about 2 minutes. Return the meat to the pan and add the oyster sauce. Stir-fry for 1 minute, then serve with the rice.

Sides

Michael Lomonaco's Quince Fruit Mustard

MAKES ABOUT 1 ½ CUPS

Though not frequently used in contemporary American kitchens, the quince was once a mainstay of home cooking in this country. Michael Lomonaco's recipe for Quince Fruit Mustard evokes the appreciation that previous generations had for the charms of this autumnal fruit. Because the quince is so tart, a great deal of sugar is added in this recipe. Cooks who find the familiar more reassuring should feel free to substitute pears but should reduce the sugar quantity by half because of that fruit's natural sweetness.

Additional flavors and textures may be added to this mustard with dried fruits such as cranberries or cherries. Add them during the cooking process and they will plump and soften.

1 pound fresh quinces (firm ripe pears may be substituted)
2 tablespoons unsalted butter
¼ cup water
¼ cup sugar (2 tablespoons if substituting pears)
¼ cup Dijon mustard

Peel the quinces, core, and cut into thin wedges.

Melt the butter in a saucepan over medium heat and add the fruit wedges to the hot butter. Sauté for 2 to 3 minutes. Add the water and sugar and bring to a boil, stirring occasionally. Reduce the heat and allow the contents of the pan to simmer for 10 minutes. Stir in the mustard and simmer for 2 minutes more to combine the flavors.

Cool completely, then refrigerate until ready to use. Use as a condiment for roasted meats, such as Michael Lomonaco's Marinated and Grilled Pork Medallions (page 185).

Jane and Michael Stern's Coleslaw

~

SERVES 4 TO 6

An all-purpose coleslaw perfect for accompanying any number of dishes. You may purchase a bag of shredded coleslaw featuring cabbage and carrots instead of shredding the first three ingredients yourself.

1 pound red cabbage, shredded
1 pound green cabbage, shredded
2 large carrots, shredded
1 cup mayonnaise
1/2 cup red wine vinegar
2 teaspoons sugar
1 tablespoon Dijon mustard
Coarse salt and freshly ground white pepper to taste
2 tablespoons finely chopped flat-leaf parsley leaves

Combine the cabbages and carrots in a large bowl.

In a smaller bowl, whisk together all the remaining ingredients. Add to the vegetables and combine well. Cover and refrigerate for at least 1 hour. Serve well chilled.

Jeanette Maier's Sautéed Red Russian Kale

~

SERVES 4

This tangy, slightly acidic side dish gets quite a workout at the Herban Kitchen in New York City. Chef Jeanette Maier recommends it to accompany lamb, hearty white fish, and countless vegetarian dishes.

Any variety of kale or leafy green, such as spinach or Swiss chard, may be substituted for the Red Russian kale.

1 tablespoon extra-virgin olive oil
6 cloves garlic, minced
1 pound Red Russian kale, stems and center stalks removed, large leaves cut in half
Water or chicken or vegetable stock, as needed
Sea salt and freshly ground black pepper to taste

Heat the olive oil in a 12-inch skillet set over moderate heat. Add the garlic and sauté for 1 minute. Add the kale and sauté, stirring continuously, until wilted, about 5 to 6 minutes. Add a splash of water if needed to keep the kale from sticking or drying out. Season with salt and pepper and serve immediately.

Michael Lomonaco's Mustard and Mint Beet Salad

SERVES 4 TO 6

This full-flavored salad dresses fresh beets with unusual ingredients to render them more complex and flavorful than they would be on their own. The mint complements the beets' sweetness. Though called a salad, this dish is served warm, not chilled.

4 cups water
1 pound beets
1½ teaspoons coarse salt
3 tablespoons unsalted butter
2 tablespoons Dijon mustard
3 tablespoons chopped mint leaves
1 tablespoon fresh lemon juice
½ teaspoon freshly ground black pepper
1 head Boston lettuce, separated into leaves, washed and dried

Bring 1 quart of water to a boil in a large pot. Add 1 teaspoon of the salt and the beets. Return to a boil, reduce the heat, and cook gently until the beets are tender, 30 to 40 minutes. (Check for doneness by sticking a sharp, thin-bladed knife into a beet. If it penetrates easily, the beets are done.) Remove the pot from the heat and allow the beets to cool completely in their cooking liquid before draining. Discard the water and slip the beets out of their skins, using paper towels to grasp the beets.

Cut the beets into ¼- to ½-inch wedges, depending on your personal taste.

Melt the butter in a small saucepan over moderate heat. Add the beet wedges and mustard and cook for 4 to 5 minutes. Add the mint and shake the pan to coat the beets well. Add the lemon juice and season with the remaining ½ teaspoon salt and the pepper. Serve on a bed of Boston lettuce, either on individual plates or on a platter.

Erik Blauberg's Pickled Vegetables

MAKES ABOUT
2 ½ CUPS

Serve these pickles with the Blau-burger (page 175) or other sandwiches.

1 European-style hothouse cucumber, cut into ⅛-inch-thick disks
1 carrot, cut into 1/16-inch-thick disks
1 cup white wine vinegar
1 cup sugar
½ cup pickling spice

Place the cucumber and carrot disks in a bowl of salted water and refrigerate, covered, overnight.

The next day, drain the vegetables, return to the bowl, and let them warm to room temperature. Place the vinegar in a saucepan and stir in the sugar. Bring the mixture to a boil over high heat and add the pickling spice to the pan. Stir to combine and return the liquid to a boil.

Pour the boiling liquid over the carrots and cucumbers. Let the vegetables stand in the liquid at room temperature until cool. Cover and refrigerate for 12 hours. Serve on or alongside the Blau-burgers.

Ira Freehof's Shredded Zucchini

SERVES 4

For any zucchini growers out there, Ira Freehof is pleased to remind us of this alternative to sautéed zucchini and zucchini bread.

3 or 4 medium zucchini, highly scrubbed
2 tablespoons coarse salt
3 tablespoons unsalted butter
1/4 cup finely diced yellow onion

Shred the zucchini in a food processor fitted with the shredding disk. Put the zucchini in a strainer over a large bowl, sprinkle with the salt, and toss to combine. Let the zucchini sit for 30 to 40 minutes. Rinse under cold water and squeeze out the excess moisture by pressing on the zucchini with a rubber spatula.

Melt the butter in a large sauté pan over medium heat. Add the onion and cook until softened, 3 to 4 minutes. Add the zucchini and stir until heated through, 4 to 5 minutes. Remove from the heat and serve hot.

Ira Freehof's Roast Garlic Mashed Potatoes

SERVES 4

These potatoes are mashed with the skins on for great taste and texture.

2 pounds Idaho or russet potatoes, scrubbed
1 teaspoon coarse salt, plus more to taste
1 head garlic, roasted and puréed (page 228)
4 tablespoons (1/2 stick) unsalted butter, cut into
    4 pieces
1/2 cup milk or heavy cream, heated
Freshly ground black pepper to taste

Cut each potato into quarters. Place in a large saucepan, add enough water to cover the potatoes, and add 1 teaspoon salt. Cover and bring to a boil over high heat. Continue to cook over medium heat for 15 to 20 minutes until potatoes are fork-tender. Drain and return the potatoes to the pot. Stir over low heat for 30 seconds to evaporate any lingering moisture. Add the butter and roasted garlic to the pan and mash with an electric hand mixer. Slowly add the milk and beat until smooth. Season with salt and pepper to taste.

Richard Sandoval's Roasted Poblanos

SERVES 4

In this recipe, chef Richard Sandoval, of Maya restaurants in New York and San Francisco, riffs on the traditional stuffed poblano, which usually features cheese and/or ground beef. Instead of serving them with black beans on the side, as they would be south of the border, he makes a purée that serves as a base for the poblano itself. Sandoval recommends the poblanos as a starter or as an accompaniment to seafood.

8 ounces black beans

7 cups cold water

2 tablespoons coarse salt, plus more to taste

2 tablespoons canola oil

4 poblano peppers

$1/2$ onion, cut into $1/4$-inch dice

3 ears corn, husked and kernels removed with a knife

2 yellow squash, cut into $1/4$-inch dice

3 beefsteak tomatoes, seeded and cut into $1/4$-inch dice

$1/4$ cup finely chopped cilantro leaves

Freshly ground black pepper to taste

8 ounces Monterey Jack cheese, grated

$1/4$ cup sour cream

Soak the beans overnight.

Place the beans in a pot with the water and 2 tablespoons salt. Bring the water to a boil over high heat, lower the heat, and simmer the beans, uncovered, for about 45 minutes until tender. Drain the beans and reserve about 1 cup of the cooking liquid.

Preheat the oven to 350° F.

Heat 1 tablespoon of the oil in a large sauté pan. Add the poblanos to the pan and pan-fry on all sides, about 1 minute on each side. Remove the peppers from the pan, place in a plastic bag, and completely seal the bag. Allow them to "sweat" for 10 minutes. Remove the peppers from the bag and peel away the skins, then cut open the peppers and remove the seeds, being very careful not to rupture the flesh. Set the peppers aside.

In a sauté pan, heat the remaining 1 tablespoon oil over medium-high heat. Add the onion to the pan and sauté until translucent, about 3 minutes. Add the corn, squash, tomatoes, and cilantro. Cook until vegetables are al dente but not soft, 3 to 4 minutes. Season with salt and pepper.

Purée the black beans in a blender with a few tablespoons of their cooking liquid until a thick paste is formed. Taste and adjust seasoning, if necessary.

Stuff the poblanos with the vegetable mixture, place in a baking dish, and sprinkle with the grated cheese. Bake in the preheated oven for about 10 minutes until the cheese is melted.

While the poblanos are baking, if the bean mixture has become cold, warm it briefly in a nonstick pan over low heat.

Spread the black bean purée decoratively on each of 4 plates, top with the stuffed poblanos, and drizzle sour cream around each pepper. Serve immediately.

John Schenk's Barbecued Onions

SERVES 4

John Schenk recommends serving this dish with almost any variety of meat, fish, or fowl. His favorite pairings are chile-rubbed pork chops, mahi mahi, swordfish, and chicken.

These onions may be served warm, cold, or at room temperature.

2 Spanish onions, peeled and cut into 1/4-inch rounds
1 1/2 tablespoons extra-virgin olive oil
3/4 cup barbecue sauce
Coarse salt and freshly ground black pepper to taste

Preheat the oven to 400° F.

Separate the onion rounds into rings. Heat the olive oil in a nonreactive, ovenproof sauté pan over high heat. Add the onions and cook, stirring constantly, for 3 minutes. Add the barbecue sauce, toss, and place in the pre-heated oven for 10 minutes. Remove from the heat and season with salt and pepper. Serve immediately or let cool and serve later.

John Schenk's Yukon Gold Potato and Horseradish Salad

SERVES 4

This potato salad has lots of zest and bite, thanks to the inclusion of lemon juice and horseradish.

2 pounds Yukon Gold potatoes, washed and scrubbed
Coarse salt to taste
2 tablespoons fresh lemon juice
2 tablespoons Dijon mustard
6 tablespoons extra-virgin olive oil
2 tablespoons freshly grated horseradish
2 tablespoons dried tarragon
Freshly ground black pepper to taste

Place the potatoes in a deep pot. Cover the potatoes with cold water. Add salt to the pot, place on the stovetop, and bring the water to a boil over high heat. Lower the heat to a simmer and cook for about 20 to 25 minutes until a small, thin-bladed knife can be easily inserted into the potatoes.

Drain the potatoes and run cold water over them until cool. Slice the potatoes into even wheels, ¼ inch thick, and place in a large bowl.

In a small bowl, combine the remaining ingredients. Pour the mixture over the potatoes, toss, and adjust the seasonings.

Desserts

Mario Batali's Peaches with Balsamic Vinegar and Black Pepper

SERVES 4

This dessert may surprise you with the use of balsamic vinegar and black pepper, two pantry staples that Americans commonly associate with savory dishes. Mario Batali fashions this recipe after the singular passion of Modena, Italy, the home of balsamic vinegar, where one is apt to find the sweet elixir drizzled over everything from Parmesan cheese to fresh strawberries. Here, the combination of balsamic vinegar and black pepper emphasizes the sweetness of the lush, fresh peaches. The ingredients are tossed together, but don't strive for an even distribution of pepper and vinegar— the desired effect is actually bites of varying intensity that leave the diner wondering what the next sensuous mouthful will bring.

4 perfectly ripe fresh peaches or nectarines
1/4 cup high-quality balsamic vinegar
1 tablespoon freshly ground black pepper
1 teaspoon sugar

Wash and dry the peaches. Cut the fruit into 1/2-inch-thick slices and place them in a large mixing bowl. Add the vinegar, pepper, and sugar and gently toss to coat. Divide among 4 martini glasses and serve.

Ray Arpke's Poached Pears with Raspberry Sauce and Soft-Peaked Cream

SERVES 4

Generally speaking, there's not much of a fall season in Florida, where temperatures often hover around 80 degrees well past Thanksgiving. But when autumn does make a cameo in the Sunshine State, chef Ray Arpke celebrates with this dessert. Many classic poached pear recipes call for orange and lemon juice in the cooking liquid, but Arpke uses a simple sugared water to keep the focus on the natural flavor of the pear, then contrasts it with a tart raspberry sauce and cool whipped cream. This sauce uses frozen fruit, acceptable here since they're being cooked down, but if fresh raspberries are in season, by all means avail yourself of them.

FOR THE PEARS:
4 Bosc pears, partially peeled in an attractive striped pattern and brushed with lemon juice
3/4 cup sugar
2 cups water, plus more as needed

FOR THE RASPBERRY SAUCE:
1 12-ounce package frozen raspberries
1/2 cup water
1/2 cup sugar
1 teaspoon cornstarch dissolved in 1 tablespoon water

FOR THE WHIPPED CREAM:
1 cup heavy cream
2 tablespoons sugar

TO PREPARE THE PEARS:
Choose a pot that will hold all 4 pears. Place the sugar and water in the pot and bring to a boil over high heat, stirring at first to keep the sugar from being scorched on the bottom of the pot. Once the water is boiling, carefully

place the pears in the water and add enough additional water to the pot to cover the pears. Cover the pot and return the water to a boil. Lower the heat and simmer until the pears are tender, which—depending on their ripeness—will take 15 to 45 minutes. When a sharp knife slides in and out of the pears easily, they are done.

Using a slotted spoon, remove the pears from their poaching liquid, allow to cool, and chill.

TO PREPARE THE RASPBERRY SAUCE:

Bring the raspberries, water, and sugar to a boil in a saucepot set over high heat. Carefully stir in the cornstarch mixture. Cook for about 30 seconds and remove from the heat. Cool and chill.

TO WHIP THE CREAM:

In a nonreactive bowl, whisk the cream while adding the sugar slowly. Continue whisking until soft peaks are formed.

To serve, place a pear on each of 4 chilled dessert plates. Top with raspberry sauce and a dollop of whipped cream.

Matt Reichel's Apple Strudel

SERVES 6

What makes this strudel unique is that chef Reichel uses cornstarch to thicken the apple filling. Reichel strongly recommends that the strudel be baked as soon as it is shaped to keep the apples from making the dough soggy. Similarly, be very careful not to overcook the apple mixture on the stovetop; the apples should retain some firmness at this stage because they will continue to cook.

2 cups apple juice
3 Jonathan or Granny Smith apples
1 cup sugar, plus more for sprinkling
1 tablespoon ground cinnamon, plus more for sprinkling
2 tablespoons cornstarch
1/4 cup water
1/2 cup golden raisins
1/2 cup shelled pecans or walnuts, crumbled into bits
5 sheets phyllo dough
1/4 cup (1/2 stick) butter, melted
Whipped cream or ice cream (optional)

In a saucepot, bring the apple juice to a boil over high heat.

Peel and core the apples and cut them into thin wedges. Place the apple wedges in the boiling apple juice. Add the sugar and cinnamon to the pot and stir to combine the ingredients. Cook the apple mixture until the apples are just cooked through but still firm, 4 to 5 minutes.

Add the cornstarch to ¼ cup water and stir to dissolve. Stir the cornstarch mixture into the apple mixture. Add the raisins and nuts and remove from the heat. Let the apple mixture cool completely.

Preheat the oven to 450° F.

Lay out the phyllo dough and cover with a damp cloth to prevent it from drying. Separate I sheet and place it on a piece of parchment or wax paper. Brush the phyllo sheet lightly with melted butter and place another sheet of phyllo dough on top of the buttered sheet. Butter the second sheet and add a third sheet of phyllo. Butter the third sheet.

Place the cooled apple mixture across the length of the narrow end of the phyllo stack. Roll the phyllo around the apple mixture and keep rolling into a log shape. Brush the outside of the log with butter and sprinkle evenly with cinnamon and sugar. Transfer on parchment paper to a baking sheet and bake seam-side down in the preheated oven until golden brown, 12 to 15 minutes. Remove from the oven and let cool. Slice and serve with whipped cream or ice cream.

Matthew Tivy's Warm Blueberry Pie with Almond Crumb Topping

SERVES 4 TO 6

In the heart of the summer, when blueberries are at their plump, juicy, explosive pinnacle, let them strut their stuff in this all-American pie. Show everyone that you used fresh ones by only baking them long enough to meld the flavors and cook the pastry. The fruit will be concealed under the topping, so be sure to remove the pie from the oven as soon as the topping is lightly browned, since this will be your only indicator of doneness.

FOR THE PIE CRUST:
1½ cups all-purpose flour
Pinch fine salt
6 ounces (1½ sticks) unsalted butter, very cold, cut into ½-inch cubes
5 tablespoons ice water

FOR THE FILLING:
¼ cup all-purpose flour
2 tablespoons cornstarch
2 tablespoons light brown sugar
2 tablespoons granulated sugar
Pinch of ground cinnamon
Pinch of ground nutmeg
1 pint blueberries
Squeeze of lemon juice

FOR THE TOPPING:
2 tablespoons all-purpose flour
2 tablespoons light brown sugar
1 tablespoon granulated sugar
Pinch of ground nutmeg
2 tablespoons unsalted butter, at room
  temperature
2 tablespoons rolled oats
¼ cup sliced almonds

Ice cream or whipped cream (optional)

TO MAKE THE PIE CRUST:
Place the flour, salt, and butter in a food processor. Pulse until the butter is almost fully mixed with the flour. Add the ice water and pulse just until the dough forms a ball. (Do not overmix or the crust will become tough.) Form the dough into 2 flat disks. (Note: You will have enough for 2 pie shells; reserve one for future use or double the filling and topping ingredients to make 2 pies.) Cover the disks separately and refrigerate for 1 hour.

Remove 1 dough disk from the refrigerator and roll it out on a lightly floured work surface about ⅛ inch thick, turning the dough as you do to ensure an even thickness. Place the dough in an 8-inch pie pan, prick all over with a fork, and return to the refrigerator for another hour.

Preheat the oven to 350° F.

Remove the piecrust from the refrigerator, cover with foil, and fill with pie weights, dry beans, or rice. Bake in the preheated oven for about 20 minutes until lightly browned. Remove from the oven, remove the weights, and allow to cool. Do not turn off the oven.

TO MAKE THE FILLING:
In a mixing bowl, thoroughly combine all dry ingredients. Add the blueberries and a squeeze of lemon juice and toss gently to combine without crushing or rupturing the berries. Set aside while making the topping.

TO MAKE THE TOPPING:
Rub all of the topping ingredients together until no visible trace of the butter remains. Set aside.

TO ASSEMBLE:
Place the blueberry filling in the baked pie shell and sprinkle loosely with the topping. Bake in the preheated oven until the topping has attained a nice golden color, 25 to 35 minutes. Serve warm, accompanied by ice cream or whipped cream if desired.

John Doherty's Irish Tiramisù

SERVES 4

Chef John Doherty created this Irish take on the Italian dessert tiramisù for our St. Patrick's Day show, substituting Irish Mist for Kahlua.

8 to 10 ounces mascarpone cheese
2 large eggs, separated, at room temperature
1/2 cup sugar
6 tablespoons Irish Mist
1 cup strong coffee or espresso
1 loaf Irish soda bread, cut into 1/2-inch-thick slices
Ground cinnamon, for garnish

Mix the mascarpone, egg yolks, 1/4 cup of the sugar, and 3 tablespoons of the Irish Mist in a large bowl with a wooden spoon. Combine thoroughly but be careful not to overmix.

Whip the egg whites, slowly adding the remaining 1/4 cup of sugar, until the mixture forms a medium-peak (i.e., just starting to set up) meringue. Fold this meringue into the cheese mixture.

Combine the coffee and the remaining 3 tablespoons Irish Mist in a small bowl. Brush the Irish soda bread with this mixture.

Cover the bottom of a soufflé dish with a layer of the soda bread. Spread one-third of the cheese mixture over the bread, then alternate layers of soaked bread and cheese, finishing with cheese. Cover and refrigerate overnight. Serve with fresh fruit and sprinkle with cinnamon if desired.

NOTE: The consumption of raw eggs carries the risk of salmonella. Foods containing raw eggs should not be eaten by pregnant women, the very young, the very old, or anyone with a compromised immune system.

Don Pintabona's Polenta Lemon Cake with Fresh Berries

~

SERVES 6 TO 8

This dessert couldn't be more simple to prepare and makes unique use of polenta. When shopping for lemons, be sure to choose bright yellow ones with a strong fragrance, both of which are good indicators of the potency of the zest.

FOR THE CAKE:
11 ounces (2¾ sticks) unsalted butter, at room temperature
1½ cups sugar
Grated zest of 2 lemons (reserve juice for berries, below)
3½ cups ground almonds (almond flour)
2 teaspoons vanilla extract
1 teaspoon lemon extract
7 tablespoons corn oil or vegetable oil
5 large eggs, at room temperature, slightly beaten
⅔ cup polenta or coarse cornmeal
½ cup cake flour, sifted
1½ teaspoons baking powder
¼ teaspoon fine salt

FOR THE BERRIES:
1 cup water
1 cup sugar
Juice of 2 lemons (see recipe in left-hand column)
2½ cups fresh berries, such as strawberries and blueberries, cleaned and sliced if necessary

Preheat the oven to 325° F.

TO MAKE THE CAKE:
Cream the butter, sugar, and lemon zest until light and fluffy. Add the almonds, vanilla, lemon extract, oil, and eggs and beat until well incorporated. Fold in the polenta, cake flour, baking powder, and salt and combine thoroughly into a homogeneous mixture. Pour into a buttered and floured 10-inch cake pan. Bake in the preheated oven for 25 to 30 minutes until a toothpick inserted comes out clean. Allow to cool for 20 minutes, then remove from the pan.

TO MAKE THE BERRY SAUCE:
Heat the water and sugar in a saucepan over medium-high heat until the sugar melts and a thick syrup is formed. As soon as the first hint of brown caramelization shows, immediately remove from the heat and stir in the lemon juice, then the berries. Spoon the berries over wedges of the polenta cake and serve.

Michael Romano's Panna Cotta

SERVES 4

The mark of a great panna cotta (Italian for "cooked cream") is that it just barely holds its shape. (Nudge an unmolded panna cotta with a fork and it should undulate voluptuously from side to side but remain intact.) Michael Romano serves his with orange sections, but you may garnish this rich little tower with other sweet seasonal fruits such as strawberries, passion fruit, or even black Mission figs.

1/3 cup sugar
2 tablespoons water
1/2 teaspoon fresh lemon juice
2 sheets gelatin or 2/3 tablespoon powdered
2 cups half-and-half
1/3 cup sweetened condensed milk
1 orange, peeled and sectioned

In a small, heavy-bottomed saucepan, combine the sugar, water, and lemon juice. Cook over medium heat, without stirring, until the sugar turns a golden caramel color, 6 to 10 minutes. Pour equal amounts of the caramel into 4 5-ounce soufflé molds. Set aside.

Place the sheets of gelatin in a bowl with ice water to cover. Stir the gelatin with your fingers until it has softened. Set aside.

In a nonreactive saucepan over medium heat, bring the half-and-half and condensed milk barely to a simmer (do not allow them to boil). Lift the gelatin sheets from the water, squeeze them dry, and stir into the heated milk to dissolve. Strain this mixture and pour equal portions of it into the 4 caramel-lined molds. Cover with plastic wrap and refrigerate until set, at least 4 hours.

To serve, carefully run a knife around the inside edge of the molds and gently invert each *panna cotta* onto an individual plate. Garnish with the orange sections and serve.

Alex Garcia's Dulce de Leche

SERVES 8

According to Alex Garcia, the executive chef of New York's Latin hot spot Calle Ocho, no one's sure where *dulce de leche* (sweet milk) originated. Some claim it began in the Caribbean; others say Colombia, where it's made by stirring goat's milk and sugar over a low flame for several hours, creating a caramelized dessert called *cajeta*, which is often spread between two thin wafers. Regardless of its origin, each Latin country now has its own version of *dulce de leche*. One of Garcia's favorite versions is the Argentinian *milhojas,* or "thousand leaves," in which the caramelized milk is spread between layers of thin, crisp puff pastry.

Here, Chef Garcia presents his own version in which *dulce de leche* is spread on crêpes and topped with fresh bananas. On our program, chef Garcia demonstrated this recipe with a modern-day shortcut— simmering an unopened can of sweetened condensed milk for several hours. While this is a tempting approach, we don't recommend that you try it at home. Instead, we've provided an old-fashioned recipe that is only slightly more trouble and infinitely safer.

FOR THE CRÊPES:
1/3 cup whole milk, at room temperature
1 cup all-purpose flour
3 large eggs, at room temperature
3 tablespoons unsalted butter, melted
1 tablespoon sugar
1/4 teaspoon fine salt
Vegetable oil spray

FOR THE DULCE AND GARNISH:
1 10-ounce can sweetened condensed milk
8 medium bananas, just ripe, sliced on a
   diagonal
Sugar, for garnish

TO MAKE THE CRÊPES:
Mix the milk, flour, eggs, butter, sugar, and salt in a blender just until smooth. Cover this batter and refrigerate at least 15 minutes or up to 1 day.

Spray a 7-inch nonstick skillet with vegetable oil spray and warm over medium heat. Pour 2 tablespoons batter into the pan and swirl to coat the bottom. Cook until the edge of the crêpe is light brown, about 1 minute. Loosen the edges gently with a spatula and carefully turn the crêpe over. Cook until the bottom begins to brown in spots, about 30 seconds. Transfer to a plate. Cover with a paper towel. Repeat with the remaining batter, spraying the pan with oil spray as needed and covering each crêpe with a paper towel. (The crêpes may be made 1 day ahead. Cover and refrigerate.)

TO MAKE THE *DULCE:*

Pour about 1 inch water into the bottom of a double boiler. Bring to a boil over high heat, then reduce to a persistent and steady simmer. Pour the milk into the top of the double boiler, set it on top of the simmering water, and cook, covered, for 2 to 2½ hours.

Remove the upper pot from the heat and beat the cooked milk vigorously with a whisk to help start the cooling process, then set aside to cool at room temperature. (It will turn a deep caramel brown and thicken as it does.) Be sure to allow the caramel to cool completely before touching, or serving, it; the hot sugar can burn!

The *dulce de leche* may be prepared 1 day in advance and kept in a tightly covered container in the refrigerator, but allow it to come up to room temperature before assembling the crêpes.

TO ASSEMBLE AND GARNISH:

Preheat the broiler.

Drizzle or spread the caramelized milk over each crêpe and place a handful of banana slices down the center of each one. Roll up or fold the crêpes so the bananas and the caramel are on the inside. Garnish the crêpes with additional banana slices and sprinkle with sugar. Heat under the broiler until the sugar caramelizes. Serve immediately.

Ira Freehof's Strawberry Shortcake

SERVES 4

Ask Ira Freehof about strawberry shortcake, and he'll give you a pep talk that inspires you to run right into the kitchen. "Forget the spongy thing you buy in the supermarket. This is the real deal." In encouraging you to make your own shortcake, Freehof appeals to our sense of time. "It only takes 3 minutes to make the whipped cream, and just 15 minutes for the biscuit!" Freehof is a man who's proud of his shortcake, damn it, and he wants you to be proud of yours, too.

FOR THE BERRIES:

1 generous pint strawberries or mixture of fresh berries, hulled and sliced

¼ cup sugar, or to taste, depending on the sweetness of the berries

FOR THE BISCUITS:

2½ cups all-purpose flour, plus more for
   shaping

½ cup sugar, plus more for coating biscuits

1½ teaspoons baking powder

¾ teaspoon baking soda

¼ teaspoon fine salt

6 tablespoons (¾ stick) unsalted butter, chilled
   and cut into 6 equal pieces

⅔ cup buttermilk

1 large egg yolk, at room temperature

½ teaspoon vanilla extract

2 tablespoons milk (approximately), for coating
   the biscuits

FOR THE WHIPPED CREAM:

1¼ cups heavy cream

1 teaspoon vanilla extract

2 teaspoons sugar

Toss the berries with the sugar 30 to 40 minutes before serving.

To PREPARE THE BISCUITS:
Preheat the oven to 425° F.

Butter a baking sheet. Place the flour, sugar, baking powder, baking soda, and salt in a food processor and pulse to combine. Add the butter and pulse until the mixture is crumbly. Place the buttermilk in a measuring cup and stir in the egg yolk and vanilla. With the processor running, add the buttermilk mixture and process until well incorporated. The dough should be slightly sticky but manageable. Transfer the dough to a floured sheet of wax paper.

Sprinkle the dough with flour. Pat the dough evenly ¾ inch thick. Using a 3½-inch biscuit cutter, cut biscuits from the dough and transfer them to the buttered baking sheet. With your fingers, coat the top of the biscuits with a light film of milk and sprinkle with sugar.

Bake in the preheated oven until light golden, 11 to 13 minutes. Transfer to a wire rack and cool for a couple of minutes.

MEANWHILE, WHIP THE CREAM:
Whisk the cream with the vanilla and sugar until nearly stiff.

Cut the cooled biscuits in half horizontally. Put the bottom half of 4 biscuits on 4 individual plates. Spoon the berries over the biscuits and the whipped cream over the berries. Cover with the top half of the biscuits. Serve immediately.

John Villa's Coconut Rice Pudding with Fresh Mango

SERVES 4

This is a highly versatile dessert with pan-Asian flavors: jasmine rice, coconut milk, and mango. Feel free to adjust the sugar to meet your own desired level of sweetness. You might also substitute pineapple, peaches, or plums for the mango to accommodate your own taste or the seasonality of these and other fruits.

3/4 cup jasmine rice or long-grain white rice
1 13- to 14-ounce can unsweetened coconut
    milk (found in gourmet markets or the Asian
    food section of a well-stocked supermarket)
1/4 cup sugar
Juice of 1 lemon
1 mango, peeled and cut into 1/4-inch dice

In a small saucepot, soak the rice for 5 minutes in enough water to cover by 1 inch. Place on the stovetop and cook slowly over moderate heat until all the water is absorbed and the rice is cooked through, 15 to 20 minutes.

In a separate pan, heat the coconut milk, sugar, and lemon juice over moderate heat until well warmed, 3 to 4 minutes. Stir in the rice, remove from the heat, and set aside to cool. Refrigerate, covered, for at least 1 hour. To serve, divide the pudding evenly among 4 bowls and top with the diced mango. Serve immediately.

Matthew Lake's Pineapple Brown Betty

~

SERVES 4

A brown betty is traditionally made with apples, bread crumbs, cinnamon, and sugar, but here chef Matthew Lake creates a summertime version using the decidedly tropical pineapple, an inspired substitution since pineapple has a great affinity with brown sugar.

If you'd like to make a traditional brown betty, substitute apple slices tossed with cinnamon and sugar for the pineapple. You could also make this recipe with pears in the fall.

2 cups milk
2 tablespoons unsalted butter
2 teaspoons vanilla extract
1¹/₄ cups (packed) dark brown sugar
¹/₂ medium pineapple, peeled, cored, and sliced into 4 ¹/₂-inch rings (8-ounce can of pineapple may be substituted)
4 large eggs, at room temperature
1 loaf sourdough bread, crust removed, ground into crumbs in a food processor (3 cups)

Preheat the oven to 350° F.

In a saucepan combine the milk, I tablespoon of the butter, the vanilla, and ½ cup of the brown sugar. Bring to a boil over high heat and remove from the heat immediately to keep it from bubbling over. Set aside and allow to cool to room temperature.

Lightly butter a small baking dish. Place the pineapple rings in a single layer in the bottom of the dish.

In a mixing bowl, beat the eggs, then slowly whisk in the milk mixture. (Be sure the milk mixture has cooled before doing so, or the heat will cook the eggs.) Soak the bread crumbs in the milk mixture for 10 to 15 minutes.

Sprinkle the pineapple evenly with the remaining ¾ cup brown sugar. Spread the bread crumb mixture evenly on top of the pineapple. Cover the dish with aluminum foil and bake in the preheated oven until set, 30 to 35 minutes. Uncover and bake until lightly browned on top, another 5 to 10 minutes. Remove from the oven and let cool. Serve at room temperature.

Erica Miller's Chocolate Banana Terrine

SERVES 4

The ingredients for this simple dessert say it all—heavy cream, semisweet chocolate, and bananas—plenty of ammunition for a potent and simple confection. It may, of course, be made with other fruits. Try those you enjoy dipping in chocolate, such as strawberries, orange sections, or cherries.

1 cup heavy cream
1 cup very finely chopped semisweet chocolate
2 ripe bananas

Special equipment: 1 terrine mold, or 4 6-ounce ramekins, greased with butter or Pam and lined with sugar and refrigerated for at least 1 hour

In a small saucepot, bring the cream to boil. Stir in the chocolate until well incorporated; it will melt very quickly. Remove from the heat immediately and cover to keep warm.

Peel the bananas and place whole in the terrine mold or cut them in half and place a half in each of the ramekins. Pour the chocolate mixture over the bananas. Allow to cool to room temperature, then refrigerate for 1 hour.

To serve, unmold the terrine and cut into 4 equal slices or unmold the ramekins onto chilled plates.

John Doherty's Warm Chocolate Cherry Crumble

SERVES 4 TO 6

Sweet, juicy cherries and bittersweet chocolate are a powerful and rich combination. When he encountered perfect specimens of this quintessential summertime fruit in the supermarket while shopping for our show, chef John Doherty devised this recipe just to take advantage of them. "As good as it was, I haven't made it since," he reports with a chuckle. Try this recipe, and see what he's been missing.

20 fresh sweet cherries, pitted and halved
2 tablespoons honey
Grated zest of 1 orange
1 ounce bittersweet chocolate, coarsely chopped
2 cups all-purpose flour
1¼ cups sugar
8 ounces (2 sticks) unsalted butter
2 tablespoons ground cinnamon

Preheat the oven to 350° F.

Mix the cherries, honey, orange zest, and chocolate in a bowl. Evenly distribute the cherry mixture in the bottom of a 6- to 8-inch pie or quiche dish.

In a mixing bowl, combine the flour, sugar, butter, and cinnamon until completely blended and beginning to gather into small balls. Break into small pieces and sprinkle the mixture evenly over the top of cherries. Bake for 20 minutes in the preheated oven. Serve warm or let cool and serve at room temperature.

Michael Lomonaco's Flourless Chocolate-Walnut Brownie Torte

SERVES 6 TO 8

This is a wonderful make-ahead recipe that may be prepared a day in advance and heated just before serving. It also lends itself to adaptation: The walnuts may be replaced by hazelnuts or almonds, and 2 tablespoons almond liqueur may be added to the cream topping to deepen the flavor. Add it along with the vanilla extract.

1½ cups granulated sugar

8 ounces (2 sticks) unsalted butter, at room temperature, plus more for buttering the pan

8 large eggs, separated, at room temperature

16 ounces good-quality semisweet chocolate, preferably French or Belgian, cut into small pieces

4 ounces walnuts, toasted and coarsely chopped (6 tablespoons)

½ cup heavy cream

½ teaspoon vanilla extract

½ cup confectioner's sugar

Special equipment: 10-inch springform pan

Preheat the oven to 350° F.

Lightly butter the springform pan. Combine I cup of the sugar with the butter in the bowl of an electric mixer and beat on medium speed until creamy yellow ribbons are formed. Still mixing at medium speed, add the egg yolks one at a time until all are incorporated. Set aside.

Melt the chocolate in the top of a double boiler over simmering water, stirring occasionally as it melts. Remove the chocolate from the heat and stir it into the butter mixture. Stir in the chopped nuts and set aside.

With the electric mixer, whip the egg whites at high speed until soft peaks begin to form. Add the remaining ½ cup sugar and continue to whip until firm peaks have formed. Stir one-third of the whipped whites into the chocolate mixture to loosen the base. Gently fold in the remaining whipped whites and pour the batter into the springform pan. Set the cake in the center of the oven and bake until a toothpick inserted into the cake comes out clean, 45 to 50 minutes.

Remove the cake from the oven and let cool for 30 minutes before unmolding. While the cake is cooling, whip the heavy cream with the vanilla.

To unmold the cake, open the hinge on the pan and run a sharp knife carefully around the pan to loosen the cake. Transfer the cake to a serving platter, dust with the confectioner's sugar, and serve with the whipped cream on top.

Robert Bruce's Un Deux Trois Quatre Cake

SERVES 4

Talk about coincidences! The building that today plays home to the New Orleans incarnation of Smith and Wollensky once housed a beloved local eatery by the name of Maylie's, a haunt that survived for more than a century. And chef Robert Bruce, the executive chef for the Big Easy's Smith and Wollensky, happens to be the proud grandson of Anna Mae and Willie, antecedents who were the fourth generation in Bruce's family to run Maylie's. In fact, Bruce himself worked there as a child.

"This recipe comes from my great-great-grandfather's business partner's wife, Madame Esparbe," says Bruce. In the late 1800s, this was actually one of the dishes on the menu at Maylie's. Though it's not offered at Smith and Wollensky, Bruce selected it for our show because of its economy.

However, the recipe's name has nothing to do with all that history. *Un deux trois quatre* is French for "one, two, three, four,"

which are the quantities of the recipe's first four ingredients.

The recipe may be baked into one large cake, as it is here, or divided among 12 cupcake molds.

1 cup (2 sticks) unsalted butter, at room
    temperature
2 cups sugar
3 cups all-purpose flour
4 large eggs, at room temperature
2 teaspoons baking powder
1 cup milk
1 teaspoon vanilla extract
Whipped cream and rum (optional)

Preheat the oven to 350° F.

In a mixing bowl large enough to hold all of the ingredients, cream the butter and sugar. In a separate bowl, beat the eggs until very light in color. Add the eggs to the butter mixture and beat vigorously to incorporate. Add the flour to the mixture and beat thoroughly again. Add the baking powder, milk, and vanilla and mix again to combine.

Line an 8-inch round cake pan with buttered wax or parchment paper and fill with the batter. Bake for 1¼ hours in the preheated oven. (If making cupcakes, bake 45 minutes to 1 hour. Remove from oven when a toothpick inserted in the center of one cupcake comes out clean.) Allow to cool, invert, remove from the pan, and slice. Serve with whipped cream and drizzled with rum if desired.

Waldy Malouf's Best Chocolate Chip Cookies

MAKES ABOUT 3 DOZEN LARGE COOKIES

There's no special technique involved in what Waldy Malouf calls the "best" chocolate chip cookies. But there is some brown sugar to provide unexpected flavor, and two extra-large eggs to help keep the dough soft after baking. There's also an inordinate amount of chips.

12 ounces (3 sticks) unsalted butter, at room temperature
1 cup (packed) light brown sugar
1 scant cup granulated sugar
1 teaspoon fine salt
2 extra-large eggs, at room temperature
1 teaspoon vanilla extract
3 cups all-purpose flour
1¾ teaspoons baking soda
2 cups chocolate chips

Preheat the oven to 350° F.

Spray a cookie sheet with vegetable oil spray. In a mixing bowl, cream the butter and the sugars together. Add the salt, eggs, and vanilla and beat to combine well. Add the flour and the baking soda to the bowl and mix until fully incorporated. Fold the chocolate chips into the dough. Place scant ¼ cupfuls of the dough 2 inches apart on the cookie sheet and bake for 15 minutes in the preheated oven. Remove them from the oven and allow to cool on the hot cookie sheet. Repeat with the remaining cookie dough. Serve while still soft.

Basics

CITRUS ZESTS

The zest of oranges and lemons can provide a powerful citrus flavor in a variety of recipes. To remove the zest, use a peeler or grater. The most important consideration is to leave the pith, or white portion, of the rind, on the fruit; it's bitter and should be avoided entirely.

ICE WATER BATH

An ice water bath is employed to "shock" vegetables, especially verdant green vegetables, after they've been cooked in boiling water. The purpose of the bath is to stop the heat retained by the vegetables themselves from continuing to cook them after they're removed from the hot water. This retains their flavor and preserves as much of their natural color as possible.

PEELING TOMATOES

It's almost never essential to peel a tomato in a recipe, but many restaurants choose to do so for a more sophisticated look to the dish. To peel tomatoes, prepare a pot of boiling salted water and have an ice water bath ready. Using a paring knife, cut a small hole at the top of the tomato where the stem has been removed. Then, slice a very shallow X across the bottom of the tomato, just deep enough to break the skin. When the water reaches a boil, carefully place the tomatoes in the water. After 30 to 60 seconds, remove the tomatoes from the water using tongs or a slotted spoon and place them in the ice water bath. As the tomatoes cool, the skin should begin to curl up, after which you may peel it off easily using your hands or a paring knife. To remove the seeds from a peeled tomato, cut off the top and gently squeeze them out.

ROASTING GARLIC

To roast a head of garlic, preheat the oven to 350° F. Place a head of garlic in a small ceramic baking dish or small makeshift vessel fashioned out of aluminum foil. Drizzle with I tablespoon olive oil and I tablespoon water and season with salt and pepper. Cover and bake for 30 to 40 minutes until the garlic cloves are soft inside their skins. Test for doneness by piercing a clove with the tip of a very thin knife. When the garlic is cool enough to handle, remove individual garlic cloves by "popping" them out of their skins. Roasted garlic may be easily mashed or puréed.

Chicken Stock

MAKES ABOUT 2 ½ QUARTS

In keeping with the spirit of this book, most of the chefs have used canned broths or included a quick stock in the recipe itself. For readers who want to make their own stock, here's a recipe for chicken stock. It may be prepared up to 4 days in advance and refrigerated, or it may be frozen for up to 3 months.

6 pounds chicken bones, roughly chopped (substitute wings if bone or carcasses are unavailable)
4 quarts cold water, or as needed
1 bulb garlic, halved crosswise
1 large onion, roughly chopped
2 small carrots, roughly chopped
½ stalk celery, thickly sliced
2 sprigs thyme
4 sprigs flat-leaf parsley
1 teaspoon whole black peppercorns
1 bay leaf

Place the chicken in a large stockpot and add enough cold water to cover by 2 inches. Bring to a boil over medium-high heat, skimming off any foam that rises to the surface. Add all other ingredients. Reduce the heat to low and simmer uncovered gently for at least 6 hours and, if possible, overnight to concentrate the flavors even further.

Strain the stock into a large bowl. Allow to cool completely. Skim off and discard the clear yellow fat that rises to the surface. (You might also refrigerate the stock until the fat chills, about 4 hours, then simply scrape it off with a large spoon.)

Who's Who in Chef on a Shoestring

DAVID AMORELLI is the executive chef at Cité restaurant in New York City. A veteran of the kitchens of such restaurants as the River Café and Park Avenue Cafe, he counts among his mentors Jacques Pépin and Cité owners David Burke and Alan Stillman. He is a proud resident of New York City and the parent of two children.

RAY ARPKE is the executive chef and owner of Florida's Euphemia Haye restaurant, which he purchased in 1980. Prior to that, he was the lead chef at a nearby restaurant.

Prior to helming the kitchen at the Knickerbocker restaurant in Greenwich Village, New York, AARON BASHY was the *chef de cuisine* at Great Jones Street's Five Points in New York City and, prior to that, executive chef at Charlie Palmer's Alva. He also cooked with Palmer at his esteemed Aureole restaurant and prior to that for the late Gilbert LeCoze of LeBernardin.

MARIO BATALI lived in Seattle, Madrid, and New Jersey before spending time in the kitchens of London, San Francisco, and Bologna. He is the co-owner and executive chef of Babbo, Lupa, and Esca—three of the most popular Italian restaurants in New York City. He is also the author of *Simple Italian Food* (Clarkson Potter, 1998) and host of two Food Network programs, *Molto Mario* and *Mediterranean Mario*.

ERIK BLAUBERG has been the executive chef of the legendary '21' Club since 1996. Prior to that, he was executive chef at SoHo's American Renaissance restaurant. In the 1970s, he worked for French legends Paul Bocuse and Roger Vergé before his first executive chef position at Colors in New York City in 1991.

JOSEPH T. BONANNO, JR. is an honest-to-goodness fireman and the author of *Firehouse Cooking* (Broadway, 1997) and *The Healthy Firehouse Cookbook* (William Morrow). He resides in Lindenhurst, New York.

JIM BOTSACOS, the executive chef of Molyvos restaurant in New York City since its opening in 1997, is a graduate of Johnson & Wales cooking school. He spent seven years at the famous '21' Club, ultimately attaining the rank of executive sous chef. He went on to become the opening chef for Park Avalon and Blue Water Grill restaurants, also in New York City.

TERRANCE BRENNAN has been the executive chef of New York City's acclaimed Picholine restaurant since it opened in 1993. The son of Annandale, Virginia, restaurateurs, Brennan began cooking at age thirteen and worked at Le Cirque, Montrachet, and Annabelle's in Manhattan, as well as the legendary Taillevent in Paris. He also worked for chef Roger Vergé at Le Moulin de Mougins in southern France. In 1990, he and his partners opened Prix Fixe in New York City's Flatiron district. Brennan lives with his wife and three children in Westchester, New York.

A native of New Orleans, ROBERT BRUCE graduated from the Johnson & Wales cooking school before returning to his hometown, where he is now the executive chef of Smith & Wollensky steakhouse. He was given the Ivy Award in 1996, the same year *New Orleans Magazine* named him Best Chef in town. He took the helm at Smith and Wollensky in 1998.

SCOTT CAMPBELL is the chef and owner of Avenue restaurant on New York City's Upper West Side. He studied at Peter Kump's New York Cooking Scool, where he eventually returned as a frequent guest lecturer, and earned his degree from Madeleine Kamman's Beringer School of American Chefs in California's Napa Valley. For seven years, he was the executive chef of Vince & Eddie's in New York City and, before that, paid his dues with stints in the kitchens of Union Square Café, Windows on the World, and Le Cirque.

JIM COLEMAN, a graduate of the Culinary Institute of America, has been the executive chef of the Rittenhouse Hotel for eight years, during which time he authored the *Rittenhouse Hotel Cookbook*. When not in one of the hotel kitchens, he hosts the PBS program *Flavors of America* and the NPR radio program *A Chef's Table*.

ALFONSO CONTRISCIANI, a native of Philadelphia, was the chef at his hometown's Circa restaurant for two years. He currently is the executive chef of the Showboat Hotel and Casino in Atlantic City. He is also the captain of the United States Culinary Olympics Team 2000.

ROE DI BONA, proprietor of Rocking Horse Café Mexicano, began her career as a visual artist. In 1988, she followed her passion for Mexican art and imagery into that country's cuisine, traveling extensively throughout Mexico. Using her artist's eye and dedicated palate to develop modern renditions of classic Mexican dishes, Di Bona has spent the last decade nurturing her restaurant, serving what the *New York Time's* Eric Asimov describes as "New York's most exciting Mexican cuisine."

JOHN DOHERTY, the executive chef of the Waldorf-Astoria Hotel in New York City, is living a culinary dream come true. When he graduated from the Culinary Institute of America in 1977, he joined the hotel's vast kitchen team and ascended to his current position in 1985. He directs 7 chefs and 120 culinarians. He oversees the hotel's three restaurants as well as a banquet operation that averages 1,000 meals a day throughout the year. He lives on Long Island with his wife and three children.

TOM DOUGLAS, a native of Delaware, began his career in the kitchen at the Hotel DuPont in Wilmington, Delaware, before heading west to Seattle in 1978. He is the owner (with his wife and business partner Jackie Cross) and executive chef of three of Seattle's most popular restaurants: Etta's Seafood, Dahlia Lounge, and The Palace Kitchen.

LINDA WEST ECKHARDT is the author or coauthor of more than a dozen cookbooks including *Bread in Half the Time,* which was named Best Cookbook of 1991 by the International Association of Culinary Professionals, and *Rustic European Breads from Your Bread Machine.* She has also been awarded the James Beard Foundation Award for Best Entertaining Cookbook. She lives in southern Oregon.

BOBBY FLAY is the executive chef of Mesa Grill and Bolo in New York City and the host of *Hot Off the Grill* on the Food Network. A graduate of the French Culinary Institute, he is also the author of three cookbooks, *Bold American Food, From My Kitchen to Your Table,* and *Boy Meets Grill.*

IRA FREEHOF is the owner of two Comfort Diners in New York City, the first of which he opened in 1996. He is a twenty-year veteran of both the front and back of the house in the restaurant business. His first industry job in New York was at the Waldorf-Astoria in 1984.

ALEX GARCIA is the executive chef of New York City's Latin hot spot Calle Ocho. At eighteen, after spending a few years working as a waiter in Puerto Rico, Garcia enrolled at Northeastern University in Massachusetts to earn a degree in hotel and restaurant management. He left to pursue a culinary education at the Culinary Institute of America and went on to complete his management studies at Florida International University. From there, he went on to work with chef Douglas Rodriguez at Yuca restaurant in Florida before following Rodriguez to New York and Patria restaurant in 1994. In 1995, Garcia took the reins at Erizo Latino restaurant and then went on to become the executive chef of Calle Ocho in 1998.

A native of Pennsylvania who was raised in Connecticut, Eleven Madison Park's executive chef KERRY HEFFERNAN was brought up loving good food and wine and began his career in the kitchen with a part-time job at age fourteen. He developed his foundation of skills with *stages* in Holland, Belgium, France, and Austria. He has cooked at the Waldorf-Astoria, Montrachet, and Mondrian, among others. His first *chef de cuisine* position was at One Fifth, a Greenwich Village restaurant overseen by Alfred Portale.

AMANDA HESSER is a staff writer for the *New York Times's* "Dining In/Dining Out" section where she reports on trends, reviews books, and covers the restaurant industry every Wednesday. Her first book, *The Cook and the Gardener,* was published by W. W. Norton & Company in 1999.

PETER KELLY is a native of Yonkers, New York. He began his career at age fourteen at a German restaurant called the Forest Haus Inn. He went on to work in many of New York's finest restaurants before making a culinary pilgrimage to France in 1983. He opened his first restaurant, Xaviars at Garrison, upon his return that same year. Today, Kelly owns four of the most esteemed restaurants north of New York City, all of them part of his Xaviars Restaurant Group. He resides in Blauvelt, New York, with his wife and son.

RICHARD KRAUSE has been the executive chef and a partner in New York City's Martini's restaurant for six years. Prior to opening his own restaurant, he spent several years cooking with the legendary Wolfgang Puck at Ma Maison and Spago in the Los Angeles area and was the original chef at Puck's Chinois on Main. He also spent one year cooking in two- and three-star restaurants throughout France.

Named one of the 10 Best New Chefs in the country by *Food & Wine* magazine in 1997, MATTHEW LAKE has been the executive chef at New York City's 27 Standard for two years.

A graduate of the Culinary Institute of America, Matthew previously cooked at New Heights restaurant in Washington, D.C.

MICHAEL LOMONACO is the executive chef/director of Windows on the World in New York City. Formerly he was the executive chef of the fabled '21' Club. In 1995, he authored the '21' Club Cookbook (Doubleday). Lomonaco is the cohost of the Discovery Channel's *Epicurious* television program and previously hosted the show *Michael's Place* on the Food Network. He lives in New York City with his wife.

For five years, JEANETTE MAIER has been the executive chef and owner of the Herban Kitchen, an organic vegetarian restaurant in New York City's SoHo district. She is a graduate of the Natural Gourmet Institute in New York City. Prior to opening the Herban Kitchen, Maier worked as a private (and sometimes traveling) chef for clients with special diets.

WALDY MALOUF graduated from the Culinary Institute of America in 1975 and has been pleasing the palates of his dining clientele ever since. Over the years, he has had affiliations with The Four Seasons, La Côte Basque, the Hudson River Club, and The Rainbow Room. In 1999, he opened Beacon restaurant in New York City. He is the author of *The Hudson River Valley Cookbook* (Addison-Wesley, 1995).

HENRY MEER is the executive chef and owner of two of downtown New York City's favorite restaurants, City Hall and the Cub Room. Prior to opening the Cub Room in 1994, he worked at the legendary Le Côte Basque for more than eight years and was sous chef to Andre Soltner at Lutece. Meer is a graduate of the Culinary Institute of America.

ERICA MILLER, a 1991 graduate of the Culinary Institute of America, has been the chef at four New York City restaurants, and is now the executive chef of Eugene, a "seasonal American restaurant" with a menu that changes every six weeks. She is a regular contributor to the Food Network.

A graduate of the Culinary Institute of America, RICK MOONEN has been the executive chef of Oceana since 1994. Prior to that, he cooked on the line at such restaurants as Le Cirque, Le Relais, and Chelsea Central. In 1997, he and his partners opened the Greek restaurant Molyvos in midtown Manhattan. He is a frequent guest on the Food Network's *Cooking Live with Sara Moulton* and CBS's own "Chef on a Shoestring."

SARA MOULTON joined *Gourmet* magazine as a food editor in 1984 and was appointed executive chef in 1987. She began her culinary education at the Culinary Institute of America, from which she graduated in 1977. She founded the New York Women's Culinary Alliance in 1982 and began her teaching career at Peter Kump's New York Cooking School in 1983. Today, in addition to her responsibilities at *Gourmet,* Moulton hosts *Cooking Live* on the Food Network.

As the director of quality control of Phillips Foods, Inc., and Seafood Restaurants, PAUL OPITZ combines his chef and seafood purchasing skills. Most recently, he spearheaded the development of Phillips's lines of FlavorRich fish, lobster, and scallop products. He also oversees Phillips's seafood-processing plants in Southeast Asia and national sales accounts for Phillips Seafoods. He is a graduate of the Culinary Institute of America and spent thirteen years as a working chef at seafood restaurants in the mid-Atlantic region and Florida.

CHARLIE PALMER opened New York City's legendary Aureole restaurant in 1988. He is a member of the James Beard Foundation's Who's Who of Food & Beverage in America and was named Best Chef in New York by the Beard Foundation in 1997. Prior to opening Aureole, Palmer was the executive chef of The River Café and received his formal training at the Culinary Institute of America. He has subsequently opened numerous other restaurants, including Charlie Palmer Steak and Aureole at Mandalay Bay Resort and Casino in Las Vegas. He also owns the Lenox Room and Alva in New York City, is a cofounder of Egg Farm Dairy, a creamery in Peekskill, New York, and is the author of *Great American Food* (Random House, 1996).

DON PINTABONA has been the executive chef of the Tribeca Grill since it opened in 1990. He is a graduate of the Culinary Institute of America and has worked with such culinary masters as Charlie Palmer and Georges Blanc. A passionate traveler, Pintabona has visited more than thirty countries and regions around the world and prides himself on bringing those influences to his kitchen. He lives in Brooklyn, New York, with his wife and two children.

LOU PIUGGI is the executive chef of the Delegates' Dining Room at the United Nations in New York City. He graduated from the Culinary Institute of America in 1983 and went on to work at The Maurise as *chef poissonier* under chef Christian Delouvrier. He has also cooked with chefs Jean-Louis Paladin and Jacques Maximin. In 1994, he began working with Restaurant Associates, who operate the Delegates' Dining Room. With RA, he shared chef duties at such restaurants as the Brasserie and at such food service operations as The Grand Tier at the Metropolitan Opera and Avery Fisher Hall. He lives in New Jersey with his wife and their four children.

After graduating first in his class from the Culinary Institute of America, ALFRED PORTALE lived in France and worked in some of its most famous kitchens. Shortly after he returned to the United States, he took the reins at the Gotham Bar and Grill. He is the author of *Alfred Portale's Gotham Bar and Grill Cookbook* (Doubleday, 1997) and *The Twelve Seasons Cookbook* (Doubleday, 2000).

DAVID REARDON, the executive chef of the Diamond Head Grill at Honolulu's W Hotel, has led a rich and varied career. He has been a member of the Texas Culinary Olympic Team since 1985, winning gold, silver, and bronze metals, and been a first-place winner in the American Heart Association Cook-Off. Prior to his position at the W Hotel, he was the chef/director of culinary services at the Orchid at Mauna Lani on the Island of Hawaii.

MATT REICHEL, a graduate of the Culinary Institute of America, is a New York native who has been cooking at the Berghoff Hotel in Chicago for five years. Previously, he spent ten years working in Rye, New York, for companies such as Pars and Flick International. He was also the executive chef of the Harris Conference Center in Glen Cove, New York, and is a certified executive chef.

CAROL RICHIE, the national volunteer spokesperson for the *American Heart Association Cookbook*, was one of the recipe developers for the book, creating 40 recipes and revising about 100 others. She is a traveling cooking instructor, television cook, and host of her own cooking show, *Cookin' with Carol*, in the Dallas–Fort Worth area of Texas.

Prior to taking the reins at New York City's four-star seafood temple Le Bernardin, ERIC RIPERT, a native of Provence, cooked under Jean-Louis Palladin at Jean-Louis at the Watergate Hotel in Washington, D.C., and with Joël Robuchon at Jamin in Paris. He became chef at Le Bernardin in 1991 and was promoted to executive chef in 1994. With the restaurant's owner, Maguy Le Coze, he authored the book *Le Bernardin Cookbook: Four-Star Simplicity* (Doubleday) in 1998.

MICHAEL ROMANO has been the executive chef of the Union Square Café since 1988. The restaurant has consistently ranked among New Yorkers' favorites in the *Zagat* survey and other dining guides. He is the coauthor (with restaurateur Danny Meyer) of the *Union Square Cookbook,* which was published by HarperCollins in 1994. Prior to joining the Union Square Café, Romano studied cooking at the New York City Technical College and worked at such restaurants as the Hotel Bristol in Paris and La Caravelle in New York City.

THOMAS SALAMUNOVICH spent a year and a half cooking in some of France's three-star restaurants after graduating from the California Cooking Academy in San Francisco, where he returned to teach some years later. He also attended Madeleine Kamman's school at the Beringer vineyards. He has cooked at Sweet Basil restaurant and opened the Larkspur Restaurant and Market in Vail, Colorado, in the year 2000.

MARCUS SAMUELSSON, winner of the 1999 Rising Star Chef award from the James Beard Foundation, has been the executive chef of Restaurant Aquavit in New York City since 1994. In 1999, he and his partners opened a Restaurant Aquavit in Minneapolis.

PILAR SANCHEZ made her debut in 1997 at the Restaurant at Meadowood, where, until 2000, she cooked what she describes as "California wine country cuisine." A native of California, Sanchez honed her craft in Paris, where she and her husband opened Café del Sol, which they operated for two years. Prior to that, she held positions at the Four Seasons Clift Hotel and Ernie's in San Francisco, the Four Seasons Baltimore, and The Wine Cask in Santa Barbara. She is currently a chef-instructor at the Culinary Institute of America, Greystone, and is featured on the Food Network Show *Melting Pot.*

The chef and owner of Maya restaurant in New York City, RICHARD SANDOVAL has been treating New Yorkers to his distinct brand of Mexican cuisine for three and a half years and began doing the same for San Franciscans at Maya San Francisco in 1999. He graduated from the Culinary Institute of America in 1992.

JOHN SCHENK is the executive chef and proprietor of Clementine restaurant in New York City's Greenwich Village. He previously cooked at such well-known restaurants as West Broadway, Mad 61, and the Monkey Bar.

JAMIE SHANNON was raised in the Jersey shore town of Sea Isle. He worked his first restaurant job at a local cafeteria, moved on to a restaurant job in Wildwood, New Jersey, and went on to attend the Culinary Institute of America. He worked for Trump Towers Hotel and

Casino before joining the kitchen team at the New Orleans institution Commander's Palace in 1984. He worked his way up the line, eventually attaining the position of executive chef.

MIKE SMITH was the original executive chef of midtown Manhattan's Blackbird restaurant when it opened in March 1999. Previously, he was the executive chef at 27 Standard in New York City and spent several years cooking under Waldy Malouf at such restaurants as the Rainbow Room and the Hudson River Club. He is a graduate of the Culinary Institute of America.

WALTER STAIB, a native of Pforzheim, Germany, has spent more than four decades in the restaurant business. He was awarded the management contract for Philadelphia's historic City Tavern in 1994 by Congress. In 1999, he authored *The City Tavern Cookbook* (Running Press). He was appointed Ambassador to the Culinary Institute of America and is the first culinary ambassador to the City of Philadelphia.

NICK STELLINO is the chef/host of the popular PBS cooking series *Cucina Amore*, which airs in the United States and internationally. He has published four cookbooks, *Cucina Amore* (Doubleday), *Glorious Italian Cooking*, *Mediterranean Flavors*, and *Nick Stellino's Family Kitchen* (Putnam). He is a major participant in PBS fundraisers nationwide and lives in Los Angeles.

JANE and MICHAEL STERN are the authors of more than twenty books about America, including *Eat Your Way Across the USA* and *Chili Nation*. They write the "Two for the Road" column for *Gourmet* magazine and "Wish You Were Here" postcards for Condé Nast's *Epicurious* on the World Wide Web.

Born in England, MATTHEW TIVY, the executive chef of New York City's Chez Louis restaurant since its opening in March 1999, was raised in Massachusetts. He graduated from the Culinary Institute of America in 1982 and has worked for various culinary luminaries including Daniel Boulud and Jean-Louis Palladin.

A Culinary Institute of America graduate, SUE TORRES began her culinary career at New York's '21' Club before becoming the first woman to work the line at La Grenouille. After serving as sous chef at Arizona 206, Torres took over the kitchen of the Rocking Horse Café Mexicano in 1997. In 2000, Torres opened Hell's Kitchen restaurant in the Times Square neighborhood of New York City.

JOSEPH TUCKER is the executive chef of Pompeii restaurant in Philadelphia.

RICHARD VELLANTE is the vice president of food operations and executive chef of Legal Sea Foods, Inc. Previously, he operated Vellante's restaurant in Milford, Massachusetts, where he earned a three-star rating from the *Boston Globe.* He studied at the French Culinary Institute in New York City, then went on to hone his skills cooking and traveling in Italy. He resides in Wrentham, Massachusetts, with his wife and two young children.

JOHN VILLA is the executive chef and co-owner of Pico restaurant in New York City. He was formerly the executive chef of the Park View at the Boathouse in Central Park and chef of JUdson Grill. He was a 1998 nominee for Rising Star Chef by the James Beard Foundation. Villa is a graduate of the Culinary Institute of America.

DAVID WALZOG cooked at the Gotham Bar and Grill and other New York City restaurants before taking over the kitchen at Arizona 206 and then Tapika and Michael Jordan's The Steakhouse NYC.

BILL WAVRIN has been the executive chef of Rancho La Puerta spa in Baja California since 1990. He was the first student of the California Culinary Academy in San Francisco to return as a teacher. He has run restaurant kitchens in northern California, Malibu, and Beverly Hills, including the Timber Hill Ranch north of San Francisco, which he opened and ran from 1985 to 1987, and served as executive chef of San Francisco's Fairmont Hotel. His association with Rancho La Puerta began when he took the job of executive chef of its sister spa, the Golden Door.

BRIAN WHITMER is the executive chef of The Lodge at Sonoma in northern California's Sonoma Valley. He was formerly executive chef of Moose's in San Francisco and, prior to that, cooked at Tavern on the Green and Montrachet in New York City.

Index

Metric Equivalencies

LIQUID AND DRY MEASURE EQUIVALENCIES

Customary	*Metric*
¼ teaspoon	1.25 milliliters
½ teaspoon	2.5 milliliters
1 teaspoon	5 milliliters
1 tablespoon	15 milliliters
1 fluid ounce	30 milliliters
¼ cup	60 milliliters
⅓ cup	80 milliliters
½ cup	120 milliliters
1 cup	240 milliliters
1 pint (2 cups)	480 milliliters
1 quart (4 cups)	960 milliliters
	(.96 liter)
1 gallon (4 quarts)	3.84 liters
1 ounce (by weight)	28 grams
¼ pound (4 ounces)	114 grams
1 pound (16 ounces)	454 grams
2.2 pounds	1 kilogram
	(1000 grams)

OVEN-TEMPERATURE EQUIVALENCIES

Description	*°Fahrenheit*	*°Celsius*
Cool	200	90
Very slow	250	120
Slow	300–325	150–160
Moderately slow	325–350	160–180
Moderate	350–375	180–190
Moderately hot	375–400	190–200
Hot	400–450	200–230
Very hot	450–500	230–260